SYNCHRONICITY AND DREAMING

-

GUIDANCE FOR OUR LIVES

RICHARD KING

GUMQUEST

Exile Bay

This edition published by Gumquest, Exile Bay 2017

Gumquest Pty Ltd
PO Box R1906
Royal Exchange NSW 1225
Australia

This book is copyright. Apart from any fair dealing for the purposes of private study, research , criticism or review, as permitted under the Copyright Act, no part may be reproduced by any process without written permission . Inquiries should be addressed to the publishers

First published as an eBook by Gumquest in 2016

Copyright © Richard King 2017

ISBN 978-1-925416-70-1 (ebook)
ISBN 978-1-925416-71-8 (paper)

Cover: Extract from painting by David Wansbrough entitled 'Totemic Image' Oil on Canvas, 1989. Author portrait by Alan Clark, 2015

Design by Hanna Gotlieb

FOREWORD

It is said that the best way to kill creativity and self-esteem in a small child is to tell it to "be quiet" to "shut up"! Yet there are many instances, too many to describe here, that an apparent difficult start to life is the 'driver' to the child creating their own non-external 'inner' dialogue; an 'out-of-body' connection to that 'other world' of mystery and guidance. I believe that this true 'gift of spirit' is amply demonstrated in Richard's case. He survived an abusive father and dysfunctional early family life; to come out on the other side as a noted and respected author and writer, a passionate patron and collector of the arts and one of life's great story tellers – a forgotten art!

In my nine years I have known Richard, I have been privileged to listen 'first hand' to many of his homilies and 'coincidences' that have strongly influenced his life's journey. I know therefore from personal experience his stories carry great authenticity, wisdom and a depth of knowing, as evidenced in this inspirational book. He writes with honesty and easy simplicity as one who has listened to and experienced the 'cause and effect'; the 'karma' of life.

'Synchronicity and Dreaming' is the pathway that Richard lays and is open to us all, if we awaken to and follow our own guiding light of synchronicity and intuition, as a valuable companion in our own personal life's journey.

Alan George Clark
Business Broker and Intuitive Palmist

DEDICATION

In loving memory of Murray Stewart Smith (1946 - 1989)

Beyond the dark – I look for you
Dear, dead friend.
Will you greet me

INTRODUCTION

This book came into being as a result of a talk I was invited to give to the Hobart Theosophical Society several years ago. It was entitled 'How Synchronistic Events and Dreams Can Shape One's Biography'. (Noting that I am not a theosophist). A few of the people present encouraged me to put [my speech notes] into writing. Others who later read the manuscript complained that I had only written about so little in my life and were craving much more detail.

This volume is not a conventional autobiography but just small glimpses of events that helped me lay a solid philosophical basis to my life and learn to 'see' clearly with compassion and understanding.

No matter how much one learns via intellect or experience, even thinking "oh I have gotten it all worked out", life will come along with a new plan. The rug will appear to be pulled from under one, testing our resolve to keep going despite life's vicissitudes. Truly a never-ending journey.

A friend told me when I was in my teens when I said to him I thought I would never achieve any sort of spiritual harmony in my life, "don't fight so called bad thoughts or perceived negative urges. Just by reading the works of advanced spiritual beings, learn how they also struggled to transform their lives". You will connect with their energy of life and they will enhance and guide you.

Don't regard anything as tainted or even 'dirty' in the conventional sense. Everything manifested in this realm is life working out its karmic symphony.

It will appear to us a horrible or even sub-human but in the grand plan all life, choices and events are part of the grand harmony of the cosmos.

All one can do is forgive those who trespass and most of all forgive one's self. The past cannot be changed. The future is created by the very 'now' of each and every minute of our days. This also seems to be the message of many illuminated souls.

So many times people who have experienced near death experiences say "I was enveloped with love; love beyond anything I can ever remember."

So I feel it is up to us to create our own destiny, observing these messages of guidance, given to us so freely by the Universe. It is our own freewill that allows us to expand our world of harmony and amazing experiences and friendship or build our own jail. Running away from events and problems (thinking we can start anew and they will disappear) they don't. They confront us in another form until we consciously face them with forgiveness and love.

Several friends over my lifetime have passed over by taking their own lives, thinking all will be resolved. In one sense it is, but until the wound has been cleaned and healed on this plane, these demons will confront us once more. To sum up; I have become (as a result of observing and listening to events) a contented and happy person. Every day I express gratitude for life, for the vicissitudes and obstacles I have experienced.

Every event has a message for us at some level. There is a lesson to be learned out of adversity that a charmed life could never achieve. The greatest music was born out of perseverance and suffering. Very little of lasting value ever emerged from a government grant or a committee. We chose to be who we are; no-one tells us to be an artist or a plumber, for example. All occupations which people toil with on this plane are their choice.

I believe one has to persevere; make mistakes and at the end of the day say to ourselves "is this what I wish to do with my life?" If it is then we will no doubt change not only our lives but also all who we come into contact with.

A wonderful journey indeed.

CHAPTER ONE

We are all born with a wonderful sense of joy and amazement at the world we have entered. Even children in totally dysfunctional homes have that before the sins of the fathers (also the mothers sometimes) are visited upon them.

They lose that innocence and harden their resolve to survive in a seemingly hostile world. Some never seem to be able to make it through those years. For a while they have that aura of sheer joy which slowly fades as they adapt to their 'conditioning'.

It seems as we age we forget where we came from or why we are here. Our lives are just a series of reactions to events and finally we end up living in a realm wholly created by our minds and environmental conditioning. It is a kind of sleep where we mechanically move about fulfilling our daily tasks etc. Some have come to call it 'The Matrix'.

Most of humanity is oblivious to the wondrous possibilities of this realm. Life can be a banquet or a famine depending upon our attitude. There are no problems posed by this world that cannot be solved by this world. I had that sense of wonder for many years and it faded only slightly in my early teens, despite a father who beat me and labelled me the 'village idiot' at every opportunity. I possibly chose this life path prior to birth hopefully to settle up some karmic debt incurred. Who knows when or where? (I pray all the accounts are now closed on that score!)

Over the centuries many religions and even whole civilisations believed in the doctrine of Karma and reincarnation.

Perhaps the people living in the western world today and possibly for the last two thousand years have forgotten our heritage of the spiritual worlds and focused all their energies developing the technology and resources of our material universe.

Of course as quantum physics evolves even more into our consciousness we will return to the concept that all mankind are spiritual beings incarnated into a physical body and not just flesh and blood alone.

Many have objected to these concepts—saying—"Well, if we have lived before why can't we remember those lives?" The truth is—many people do and there are thousands of documented cases investigated by interested parties, who were able to verify details given mostly by children up to the age of five or six. After that time the shutters on that window close and the child focuses upon the day to day events of this world and their own biography.

We forget the one thing most important for every soul coming into this realm. They come with a clean slate. No one knows or remembers who they were previously. I call this "the great gift of forgetfulness." If we and others remembered our past lives we would never be given that opportunity to undo the evil we created, balance the karmic books and evolve towards our future potential, using our own free will.

Every one of us is totally unique in this universe. We all may have similar experiences, but no two experiences are the same. Our life experiences and attitudes determine how that experience is played out and assimilated into the golden garment we weave during each lifetime. We call it the soul or maybe it is even a totally new body we are creating for us to inhabit at a future time.

I feel our lives are of infinite possibility and as we have free will it is our choice as to the road we follow or create. It has been said "there are many roads which lead to Rome" but I feel there are no restrictions as to the path we choose or hack out of the jungle of adversity that may be blocking the way for us. That said, I hope the reader will be interested enough to hear about a journey I embarked upon over three score and ten years ago.

Born in a small private hospital in a western Sydney suburb I recall those first five years as perhaps the happiest of my life, despite whooping cough and other events.

Everything was an adventure—the train rides to the city with my mother, the ferry rides across the harbour to Manly for swimming and visits to the zoo at Mosman.

All stand out in my memory as wondrous, fantastic events. It was not just the outer world that was a constant joy and adventure for me. I also lived in a realm of dreaming at night. These dreams were both scary and sublime.

The sublime ones featured many foreign lands where I would fly over wondrous landscapes, watching people on the ground going about their lives. These dreams were often in serial form also! The bedroom when dark would be full of people sitting around chatting or knitting, etc. Every period of history was represented by the garments they were wearing. I never mentioned these phenomena to anyone as I felt, perhaps, they also may have experienced such events.

One evening a 'skeleton' shaped visitor arrived and upset all my so called invisible guests. Much agitation and yelling ensued, so I took control of the event and ordered them all to leave. They left and never returned.

It was as though something inside of me made a decision to close that door to other dimensions and to focus on this realm alone.

I did continue to dream in episodes until I was about six or seven. I would return from school to say to my mum that I wanted to go to bed to find out what happened in the next episode of my dreams. Of course she was always chastising me about having too much 'imagination' and refused to let me go to bed.

By the time I was eight all these wonderful dreams stopped. I was always doing shopping after school and often preparing dinner for my siblings and Grandmother and, of course, parents, as mum suffered from frightful migraines and would be confined to bed for several days at a time.

My sisters being older were either working or at high school so unable to do these chores. One learns very quickly to adapt to life's obligations.

There was one dream that occurred repeatedly over many years, well into my thirties. It has had some interesting manifestations over the years.

It began with a large gathering of people enjoying a party with dancing in a large room of an early 1900's style home. The rug had been rolled back, revealing a parquet floor in herringbone pattern.

The room had gently curved walls with large French doors opening on to a terrace which was lit by burning flares on pillars leading to a pool. Most people had stopped dancing and the band had, I presumed, gone for a break, when a group of men in masks (I think of animal heads in a rubber material) burst into the room and started firing machine guns.

I jumped behind a curtain on the door and everything went blank. The guests were attired in the fashions of the early 1920's, so I am assuming that was the time it happened. At that time, I seem to be a young boy of about twelve years old.

This dream when I was very young caused me much distress and I would wake up screaming. Later I started to 'observe' about features in the dream and got more and more detached from the trauma of it all.

The local cinema would often show black and white 'shorts' (as we called them) prior to the main feature at the Saturday afternoon matinee.

When I was about eight or nine they showed a documentary of the 'hidden' side of the city of Philadelphia in the USA.

As the camera wound its way down a street, highlighting the grand mansions tucked away behind high walls and hedges I 'knew' what was going to be shown in the next street, then the next street and so on. All was as I 'remembered'. I began to cry as I felt I was 'home'. In my mind's eye, I can still see those streets to this day.

My feeling later on was that the house I died in all those years ago must have been in Philadelphia as I felt such a connection to it. Many years later however I was told by two psychics that in fact the home was in New York City almost around the site of the World Trade Centre and 'Little Italy' (as it is known) not far away.

Both explained to me the bullet had been meant for my father but had taken me instead. In fact the bullet had taken both of us. My father had been involved with 'bootlegging' during the Prohibition era and had fallen foul of the Mafia. It seems my mother had left him earlier and moved to Philadelphia to where her parents lived. She did not like my father's Mafia links. Hence my connection with that city.

Apparently Italian, only, was spoken in the New York home and when I was in my teens (in this life) I started evening classes in Italian. I did not know why but just felt I needed to speak the language!

The lessons I learned in that brief life have held me in good stead many times when I could foresee unwanted consequences down the track. I would intuitively know to change direction. I have avoided assiduously, violent movies involving similar scenarios.

I taught myself to read when I was four by looking at the printed words in a book as my sisters read to me. By five I was able to read anything I wished. So opened another door to that glorious inner world of imagination. No wonder the Nazis burned books. They hated free thinkers

CHAPTER TWO

It has been said, "what comes out of our mouths defines us much more than what goes in." There is no doubt in my mind "we are what we think". An incident which took place when I was five years old altered so much in my life from then on.

My mother was pregnant with my brother — it was 1948. I had never seen my father drunk or abusive up to that time but one evening he came home from work and was very violent towards my mother to the point of striking her, causing her to fall on the kitchen floor. I turned to him and said, "if you ever hit my mother again I will kill you."

From that time forward we never saw eye to eye on any subject whatsoever. I still craved for a father's love but it never came.

About thirty-five years later I had a dream. I was in a room totally lined with pine boards; even the ceiling. There were windows very high up which opened out from the top. Internally there were wooden shutters on each frame. It was like a medium sized hall. Beside me was a figure in a greyish type of robe. Someone I seemed to know. I said, "there is a ghost trying to get into the room. We must shut the windows as ghosts cannot pass through glass." We both climbed up, closed all the windows securely and then the shutters which were also bolted.

For a moment all was still. Then one could see all the screws which were holding the hinges in place start to unwind simultaneously. The shutters fell to the floor and every window flew open. The ghost came in and said in a loud voice: "there is a camera hidden under that floor board. The film is still in it from 1948. On it is an image of the man who killed me and I want his forgiveness!" I turned to my mentor and said, "why would the victim of a murder want forgiveness from the murderer?" My mentor knelt down slid the board back and there was the camera. He took it into another room to develop and print the film. When he returned the images were of myself first and the murder victim — my father! I said to my mentor, "I was five years old in 1948 and secondly — my father is still alive, so I did not kill him!"

Then I awoke.

Pondering the dream, I realised my thoughts behind the words I had uttered all those years ago had indeed killed some part of my father — and even though he was still alive and we were by then OK in each other's company, I realised part of him wanted closure so he could heal and move on with his life.

So many of us are scarred by our upbringing and instead of letting it go we harbour thoughts and feelings of resentment for the rest of our lives. Hopefully all I experienced in those twenty-one years living with my family are now laid to rest for good.

In those early teen years I was fascinated by stories of ghosts, UFO's and all sorts of occult phenomena. I had read books by George Adamski and boldly took it upon myself to write to him about my inner experiences and his philosophical approach to life. He wrote back and I received several marvellous letters over the next few years. When I was about sixteen, I was able to meet him during his Sydney lecture tour.

I was always drawing diagrams of solar systems etc and one day at high school a friend grabbed one of them and said, "'Spooks' would like this." I said, "Who is 'Spooks'?" He replied "Mr Roberts the science teacher". I did not know him as there were several science teachers at the school. With me in hot pursuit he raced to his class room where the teacher was alone, reading and eating his lunch. He dropped the map in front of him and said, "Look what Richard has drawn." He said, "Oh that is fine. Everything is as it should be. Wait—what is this little disk-shaped object and the dotted orbit you have circled?" I said "Oh George Adamski told me such and such." He replied, "You know George Adamski"? (His books were best sellers in the 1950's). I said. "Yes, he writes to me every so often from California." Mr Roberts said, "I have a small study group and we discuss subjects like this. Could I borrow the letters to show them?" I replied, "Yes, as long as they are returned." Which they were and so began a life altering, lifelong friendship. His influence in my life is still with me today.

For the next three years at high school I spent every lunch hour with him discussing the philosophies of some of the world's great thinkers. The work of Max Heindel was the first adept who entered my life. His writings were like manna from heaven for my soul. They clarified so much that I had 'known' but had been unable to articulate in my mind. The book was about eight hundred pages long but I read it several times. This led to Rudolf Steiner, Helena Blavatsky, Emanuel Swedenborg, Gurdjieff, The Gnostic Gospels and many others who had trode their own road. Joan Grant's novels were devoured as were many, many more who were writing about their life experiences at that time.

I started going to the lectures at Adyar Hall in Bligh Street Sydney, owned by the Theosophical Society. I was twelve at the time and one member said to me "where's your mother little boy?" I explained I was on my own which no doubt was a surprise for her. As I write we are still friends to this day. Even though she is in her ninetieth year she is still very sharp and conversant with modern technology.

These synchronistic meetings do indeed shape and guide one's life in all its twists and turns. I feel all these 'friends' do not happen by chance and we have connections going back many lifetimes. We almost seem to be able to pick up from where we left off—all those centuries ago. Eric Robert's friendship continued after I left school at fifteen (we corresponded for several years).

Despite protests (the headmaster had wanted me to graduate etc) I was told by my parents, no, that I had to get out and earn a living which I did, as an apprentice carpenter for a few months until the bank manager offered me a job which I accepted. I met a mutual friend of Eric Roberts in the bank at Manly. He and I became constant friends and one day as I was eating my lunch I said, "you're a friend of Eric Roberts!" He said, "how did you know that?" I replied, "I just knew!" So opened another door. There was a tiny church in Chatswood called Liberal Catholic Church of Saint Frances. For many years I used to walk my cocker-spaniel dog 'Susie' by there and wonder what happened inside.

With no self-esteem — all destroyed by my father's constant brutality — I was never game enough to front up myself. My banker friend (Crosbie Wilson) told me Eric Roberts and his wife Pat used to go there (as he did) each Sunday. So again something I was interested in pursuing was granted.

From early 1960 and for the next ten years I was very much involved with the church. It resonated with so much within me (even being asked to give sermons, etc). As I was so shy it took a lot to get me behind the lectern. Re-reading these talks today I am surprised what I seemed to 'know'!! Again I think I was overshadowed by a guiding force. I met some wonderful people who became lifelong friends. They were days of much enthusiasm indeed.

I had taught myself basic yoga in my early teens and was privileged to be taught later on by Michael Volin and Nancy Phelan—two of the founders of Yoga in Australia.

But I have gotten ahead of myself a little. There were minor happenings in my youth, upon reflection, showed me how inter-connected we all are — that is the people who are on our wave length and the oracles who speak to us every day — but we are too preoccupied to notice.

At a Cub night when I was about ten years old I arrived late to be greeted with rubber mats all over the hall floor and parents of the cubs sitting around the perimeter. As I walked in the cub master said "OK King you're next!" Not having a clue what was going on I was confronted with a huge guy charging towards me! Something inside me got very angry. Instinctively I touched his nose with my finger, made a circle in the air and to my and everyone else's amazement, he followed my finger, did a complete somersault and landed flat on his back. Not a sound came from the parents as I walked out the door. I never returned.

Possibly because of my father's neurosis I have resented anyone imposing — or trying to impose — their authority upon me. I believe all of us should take responsibility for our own lives. To be as self-reliant as possible; never imposing our will upon others or harming nature, animals and our fellow human beings.

Leonardo de Vinci is reported to have said, "one day mankind will come to look upon the killing of animals — whether for sport or food — with the same horror we view the killing of fellow human beings. Also we will cease to be the walking grave yards of their slaughtered bodies."

Living in a house of meat eaters was difficult but from my late teens until I left home at twenty-one, I tried to eat as little as possible. I had promised Eric Roberts that I would stay until I was twenty-one to nullify any karmic debt I owed my father.

As I mentioned previously hidden forces within our souls — possibly learned thousands of years ago — will surface when the need is there.

My father raised his arm to strike me once when I was about fifteen. I heard a voice arise within me and instinctively raised my hand to point at him. The voice — not mine — I'm sure as it was so deep said, "Stay!" His arm froze in mid-air and he walked from the room with his arm still raised. What he said to my mother (I know not) but I did notice a more subdued attitude for a while. Goodness knows what went on there. Was it an echo from a bygone era when sounds were used as very forceful weapons or aids to construction?

There are many legends of huge stones weighing so many tons. No crane is available even today to lift such stones and yet they are in place so tightly; not even a sheet of paper could be inserted. These stories come from Ancient Egypt, South America and even parts of Asia. The legends say key notes of the stones are found enabling them to float. Coral Castle in Florida is a recent enigma of the practice.

Chanting used in meditations would also fit into this category.

Fifteen must have been an important year for me as I also had an experience of waking up outside my bedroom window about 2 am. It was a clear moonlight night. At first I was concerned I had died as I could see my body on the bed. Closer inspection revealed I was still breathing and I could see this fine silver cord connecting 'me' to it.

The feeling of elation was profound. I decided to 'fly' up to the clouds where I could see the city, the ocean, the mountains — everywhere I looked was so energising and thrilling. I kept telling myself "be careful or you will wake up!"

Then I glided down to our back garden which was very large and as I 'flew' between an orange tree and the side fence I was confronted by a large spider web. Firstly I thought "yikes", then just as quickly, I thought, "no worries"; I'm not physical, so it won't cling to me. I then started to rise up into the night sky once more and, bang — I was awake in my body on the bed once more. There have been several times this has happened since but that first conscious realization of my being in control of my thoughts and what I wanted to do is forever etched in my mind.

In the morning I inspected the orange tree and sure enough there was the spider web as I remembered it.

CHAPTER THREE

Throughout these teenage years I suffered all the usual problems young men go through as they mature. There is guilt — lack of confidence in one's self and many more hang-ups too numerous to mention. All very important and horrible for me at the time. My acne was so bad the bank paid for medical help! Of course it was all caused by the stress constantly created at home by my father. These facial eruptions started in my early teens and continued until I was twenty-one and within a couple of weeks of leaving home they completely cleared up.

At thirteen I heard the glorious violin music of a master for the first time, David Oistrakh. Years later I once jokingly said to a friend in the music world "David Oistrakh ruined my life"!

In a sense it was the complete opposite but I did go down a tortuous road for many years as a result of hearing him play at the NSW State Conservatorium of Music. Again it was just an hour or so of amazing music that opened up another world for me.

He staged a special concert for school students and I was lucky to be able to go at a cost of four shillings a ticket. He commanded much more than that at the main Town Hall recital. I had never heard anything like it in my life and at the age of thirteen was desperate to learn to play a violin.

The music teacher at school said he would teach me if I had my own instrument. Having no idea how much money one would need I asked my mother if she would buy one. "No" was the direct answer; even though the one pound a week I earned as a delivery boy at the chemist shop was taken by her for board, bus fares to school and clothing. I was left with two shillings for over twenty hours work a week.

It was only when I had left school and was in Brisbane at my sister's home I was able to buy one for eight pounds. I found a teacher, Miss McGilchrist, in the old Palings Building in Sydney and so began years of torture as I had left it far too late to master such a difficult instrument. Lacking confidence in myself also did not help much.

The plus side was that music opened so many doors to so many wonderful loving people and their homes. I discovered the music of Bach — Mozart — Beethoven and many others. However the Master for me was Richard Wagner.

I had read when I was young the myths and legends Wagner had based his music dramas upon and when I finally did hear the music on record for the first time; all fitted like a glove. His music is very special and, I feel, important for mankind at our stage of evolution.

To experience the Ring Cycle and Parsifal in the right setting — production and mood — one is transformed at a soul level and even at a physical level. I feel his works are a guiding light for mankind in his descent and ascent on his spiritual path. In this materialistic age man needs to remember his spiritual heritage otherwise materialism may take over.

Without these amazing gifts to Mankind I feel there is a huge danger he could descend into an almost sub-human level. So many people today scoff at this suggestion but through my own experiences I know there to be an element of truth in it all. I am at a loss to understand how we can look at the wonder of the human body — its beauty — its methodology etc, and say that it's all just chance! A few cells that started in slime and divided and evolved into us!

Of course each of us is master of our ship and we determine by the set of our sails the way the ship goes; not by the way the wind blows! We have always the free will to make or break our own lives. It is no use always blaming others, as out of every adversity we encounter some new thinking, some new impulse often very positive that would have lain dormant had we not gone through that particular ordeal.

When one thinks about it, some of mankind's greatest gifts of literature, music and art have come from individuals who suffered great adversity in their lives.

Nothing of great value to man has ever come out of a committee or a government grant. Individuals do change the world for better or worse.

By 1966 I had found a job with BOAC as their accountant in Australia and was able to travel to Europe, Asia and America. Again new doors opened and again I was absorbing so many amazing possibilities in life.

That has always been my problem. The cornucopia of life is so abundant—there is so much to find in joy and fulfilment I could never understand how anyone could be bored for a moment.

The bank had been my life. I knew its workings at a branch level from manager down. I really loved it and got on so well with the customers and fellow workers. My intuition with regard to who was trustworthy and who was not always held me in good stead. My intuition was never wrong.

But the urge to travel was huge and as I was so poor the opportunity provided by this opening with the airline was too good to pass. Again music was central to my life and I attended so many wonderful concerts, recitals and operas both here and abroad.

I joined the English Wagner Society hoping to get a seat at the Bayreuth Festival and had applied for many years with no results. Finally I did succeed through a friend at Lufthansa and was able to go in 1977 for the first time.

As I said — to experience these music dramas in their true home and setting was like an initiation into a special realm. I went again in 1979.

The following year a man who was going for the first time asked me about it my experiences there. The reservations assistant at Lufthansa had told him to talk with me as I had already been twice. I said to him, "Why don't we start a Wagner Society in Australia?" He was overjoyed at the thought of it and I suggested obtaining a copy of the British group's constitution etc and we could model it from there. He did and today the Society is still flourishing with many hundreds of members. Groups have also formed in most mainland states. All play an important role in furthering the work of Richard Wagner; in the form of scholarships and sponsorships, etc.

So again from that one concert by David Oistrakh all those years ago so much has blossomed and brought forth so many positive, wonderful outcomes for so many artists, musicians and music lovers all over this continent. Who knows if any of this would have happened, had I not attended that concert on a Saturday afternoon in 1956.

It is not unlike the stone thrown into a still pond, sending ripples in all directions. One never knows how far the strength of that ripple will carry and what effect those changes to the surface of the once still pond will have on all that is touched.

CHAPTER FOUR

In the late 1960's David Jones Department store had their food hall in the George Street store near Wynyard station. They made excellent sour dough bread and I would often call on my way home from work to buy a loaf.

The queues would make their way out of the basement up the stairs and often into the street.

This particular evening about 5 pm I walked in to find no other customers waiting! I remarked to the middle aged woman how odd this was. She said "We were all just saying the same thing."

By some extraordinary circumstances (I had never spoken to her before) she was telling me how horrible her mother had been to her all her life! I 'heard' myself asking her, "is your mother still alive?" The answer being, "no," I then heard myself telling her what she must do!

"This evening—find a space where you will be alone and unheard. Place two chairs facing each other and sit in one."

"Say, Mum I want to talk with you. Please sit in this chair opposite me. Firstly say — out loud — mum I know I was not always the child you wanted me to be and I ask your forgiveness. Secondly — I know we hardly ever saw eye to eye on anything and I suffered very much as I just wanted your love and support."

"I do forgive you for all the horrible things you did to me as I hope you will also forgive me. I want to move on with my life and also I want you to find peace and happiness wherever you are now. Again I do forgive you with all my heart as I hope and pray you will forgive me."

The woman said, "are you a psychologist?" I replied, "no, I don't know where all that came from! It does seem, though, to be good advice as I can see you are letting your mother rule you from beyond the grave. If she appears to have destroyed the first half of your life — why let her destroy the last?"

Having paid for the bread, I said goodbye and as I was walking out there seemed to be masses of people entering the store.

Three weeks later I was again buying bread when the woman in question rushed up to me to say she had done as I suggested and she had felt a huge weight lifted from her soul. She said, "I feel so free now." I replied, "Yes, your mother orchestrated the whole thing. Somehow — I don't know how — but she kept all these commuters out of the store so you could speak with me and perhaps she put the advice I gave you into my mind. She wanted peace and forgiveness and was trapped in a realm where she was experiencing all the pain she inflicted upon you. By your granting her wish she is now free, as you are too!"

This type of dialogue has happened to me on many occasions. Just recently I bumped into the son of an old friend whom I knew was very sceptical of anything to do with afterlife, etc. I asked after his mother and he told me she had died a couple of years previously.

Instantly I heard myself telling him about something only he and his mother would have known about and the colour drained from his face. I have no idea now of what I said — but he said to the friend he was with, "we have got to go now." And he almost ran off.

No doubt his mother had spoken through me as a way of getting her son to realise she was still very much alive in another realm and was keen to get him to open up his mind to the wonders waiting to be explored, if he would just accept the spiritual into his life. People like him find it very difficult when they cross over. For a long time they can be 'lost' in a realm where all their concepts do not work anymore.

It seems often they cannot be helped until they ask. Always our free will is respected by the beings that assist us through these transitions. Also from what I have gleaned observing these trapped beings over the years I see they are clothed in garments from almost every period of earthly history. So some must have been trapped there for many, many centuries.

This research is supported by the work of The Monroe Institute in USA. One of their programs is to train people whilst still living on this plane to try to help these lost souls.

Free will is fundamental to life at every level of existence. Sometimes people confuse licence for free will, hence free will does not impose any restrictions or pain on others — including the sentient beings co-existing with humanity on this Earth.

My grandmother on my mum's side of the family had been lady in waiting to Lady Violet Munro of Clan Munro based at Foulis Castle in Inverness Scotland. She had three women to assist her as her role was to accompany Lady Munro to all official events and for three months of the year, 'The Season', in Paris.

Grandma was a wonderful seamstress and made all the gowns for her ladyship. At the end of the season they were given to Gran and she altered them to fit herself. Lady Munro could not be seen in last year's clothes!

When my mum was four her family emigrated to Sydney where they seem to have flourished, building their own home in Lane Cove and also a thriving kiosk business near Palm Beach (the latter forced to close during the Depression).

My Grandfather died before I was born and Gran always told me when I was young "he always told me, 'Maggie — die in your own bed.' "

When I was about sixteen my mother phoned me at work to say Gran had died at five minutes to two pm. The ambulance was due at 2 pm! I said "Oh mum — she got her wish —she died in her own bed!"

Three or four weeks after she passed I dreamt she was sitting in a lounge chair. I said, "Gran what are you doing here?" Her reply was, "No one hears me — no one takes any notice of me — no one brings me food." I said, "Gran, you died. What are you still here for?" She told me not to be ridiculous and would not believe me at all. Then I awoke.

Another week or so went by and again the dream seemed to pick up where it left off. Again she protested at the rudeness of people ignoring her. I said "Gran I will prove to you — you are dead! Come on, we will go to the cemetery."

In an instant we were there and with my hand I folded the earth and grass back like a blanket. The coffin was clearly visible. I said, "Gran I will open the lid and all that will be left will be the remains of the garment you wore whilst on Earth."

I did this and it was a horrible mess of worms, etc. This seemed to convince her and I told her, "Come on — I can take you so far but not over to the other side — just to the edge. Grandpa will be waiting for you."

We walked up a beautiful grassy slope. Along the horizon was a light of the most beautiful quality. I gave her a hug and she walked into the light and turned and waved to me as I saw a hand clasp hers and guide her through into one of the many mansions — or dimensions —of life.

CHAPTER FIVE

Don't think my life was all plain sailing as there have been many many challenges in my life. Sometimes I think I have tried to resolve too much for one lifetime; but when one compares one's life to others who have survived concentration camps and almost every adversity that life could throw at them — then perhaps I have had a charmed existence!

As I have said, our attitude to events determines if the experience will make or break us. I have always felt privileged as I have always had an inner certainty of the unlimited possibilities of life.

A solid philosophical foundation has seen me through some dire times. My experience has led me to believe — find your own path — attend lectures by gurus, advanced souls, great minds —be inspired but always try to make your concepts of life your own. As long as I always say—they do not impose restrictions on any other person or sentient being.

My observations — reading — thinking and feelings led me to regard the sweep of history in thousands of years. The everyday in a sense became insignificant when compared to man's evolution as a spiritual being dipping his toe in the waters of the material world. It often enabled me to rise above issues which appeared petty to me but monumental, perhaps, to others.

I have been blessed with wonderful dear true friends for most of my life — people who have stood by me through the good and the bad. Sadly as many were older they have passed over. Others, perhaps, died well before they should have.

My partner and I purchased a semi-detached home in Mosman in 1970. It had two bedrooms. The first bedroom was used as a workroom for my picture framing, etc. Our cat, 'Wicka' would never venture into it, always using another way to meet us in the courtyard.

It was a deceased estate when purchased. The owner we found out later had died in that front room. She had lived alone there for forty years and apparently was a very lonely woman, as we learned later.

Every morning six bobby pins would be found in the hallway! Each night the hall was inspected to check none were there and we even suspected the cat might have found a pile of them under the house and brought them inside.

Later on we came to realise it was our past owner of the house. Each night at 10 o'clock sharp one would see out of the corner of the eye a figure glide through the lounge into the hallway. The room temperature would drop as well. Even guests would suddenly exclaim, "who went through that door?" It was always 10 pm.

One evening after about a year of sudden temperature drops with by now an abundance of bobby pins I resolved to confront her.

I addressed her as she made her nightly visitation and asked her to stay awhile. I explained what we were doing to the house, etc. I told her she could stay if she wished — but no more bobby pins! I also explained to her that she had died, and that loved ones were waiting for her on the other side beyond that wall of light.

Two nights later I was awoken by a violent shaking of the bed. One could see hand imprints in the doona, pushing up and down in sets of six. Again, the six had something to do with six bobby pins. What? I had no idea.

A picture came into my mind: our cat was sick in the kitchen. Upon inspection it was as I had seen in my mind's eye. I think she was telling us she was aware of her state of being and it was a goodbye and thank you. We never had another bobby pin or saw her again.

The cat loved that front room from then on and would curl up there often to sleep as I worked there.

My friend from the 1950's who had asked where my mother was at the Theosophical talk, had begun these weekend courses to 'awaken abilities within oneself' not common in most people. Today some would call it 'remote viewing' or 'biofeedback'; a course in exploration of our unlimited potential.

It was 1971 or 72. Another dear friend had done the course and she urged me to try it but I was dubious as I thought it might be a bit of a con created to make money. However I could not reconcile such a scenario if my Swiss theosophical friend was involved as she is a woman of the finest integrity.

I went along to her home one evening where past students explained to interested parties what they had gotten from it all.

I was introduced to a young man from Samoa who said, "give me the name of someone you know who is unwell, their age and the suburb they live in."

I gave him the name of a work colleague who had retired early due to depression of a very severe nature.

Our Samoan was spot on in every aspect of his problems and personality, etc. He added, "his left shoulder is very painful and he has suffered from it for some time." I knew nothing of this but said, "can you send him some healing?" He did. The next morning I phoned Adrian whose first comment was, "oh I have been meaning to phone you but I have had such agony from this shoulder—it has been horrible." He then went on to say that about 8.15 the previous night the pain disappeared and he slept the whole night through for the first time in months.

I never mentioned to Adrian anything about the healing, etc. No need to burden people with new concepts.

Needless to say I did do the course and thought at the end of it — if I had learnt nothing else I had learnt the power of positive thinking.

Basically it was a method where one learnt to release one's mind and body — visualizing colours and stairs leading down into imagined rooms underground. It was designed to align one with the deeper levels of sleep whilst still being wide awake. Rapid eye movement was a good indicator one had achieved the desired state of consciousness.

At the end of the course we had a vegetarian meal in the conference room where we had practised. I was introduced to a former student who gave me the name of an elderly gentleman friend who was very unwell. I told him I could not see anything at all. He said, "tell me what comes into your mind." I replied "all I keep seeing is a pergola covered in wisteria." "That is right," he said. "What else?" "Oh there is an old man in a wheel chair there and he has had his legs amputated—oh he is a very cranky fellow." He confirmed I had described him exactly. I then went on to describe someone in the final stages of diabetes—something about which at the time I knew

next to nothing. "Oh, (I added) his liver is in a very sick state." "Oh no," said the gentleman, "his liver is fine according to the doctor." "No," I replied, "it is very bad."

Another young man's name was given to me by someone else and I 'saw' all the problems he was going through; petty crimes etc plus some sexual problems as well. I could see he had a very authoritarian father but I could also see he would be OK in the future.

What was remarkable to me, most of all, I was completely non-judgmental. One could understand why he was the way he was and I got the distinct impression perfect justice did rule the world. Even though the evidence before our eyes of the daily events of people destroying other lives and whole nations at each other's throats — there was an order underlying it all. Something far beyond our present understanding.

A week or so later I was again at Celia's home and the gentleman who mentioned the man with diabetes and the legs amputated had mentioned to his doctor he should have the liver re-examined. At first the doctor refused but after much encouragement he agreed. It turned out exactly as I had 'seen' it.

The extraordinary outcome of this course was the 'graduation' dinner a few weeks later.

There were several other groups headed by different teachers. Celia's groups were the only groups who displayed any sense of love for the welfare of their fellow man. All the other groups had been keen to use these skills to enhance their material wealth and success. There was very little about them that one would say was spiritual.

It was a real eye opener for me as I always felt when one was able to source these powers one had to be of a special spiritual nature. I realised because we have free will, everything we touch in life can be used for positive or negative outcomes. We can all make or break our lives by our attitudes and respect or lack of, for our fellow travellers.

Over the next few months a group of us would gather on a weekly basis to talk about our experiences and at the end of the evening send healing to anyone we knew who was in need. In our mind's eye we would form a vortex of white light and just say out loud the name of the unwell person.

That very day a woman friend I knew who had a small art gallery had been operated on for a tumour removal from her breast. This was the third time over several years that this had happened. I said her name — nothing more.

Next day I phoned her at the hospital and she told me, "I'm the talk of the ward." "Why," I enquired. "Oh, they are going to take the stitches out today as everything has healed up overnight! All there is, is a pink line." I said nothing about our healing group and several years went by.

One morning I met up with her by chance at an art auction and she said, "I know you like that particular artist's work — I won't bid against you." For which I thanked her. I duly purchased the two works and just prior to paying for them I said, "Have you ever had a reoccurrence of the cancer?" "No, never." she said. I then, very stupidly, said, "Oh, our healing group must have done a very good job." (I had only ever said her name once). She flew into a rage and said, "how dare you do such a thing." I was stunned. I felt sick in my stomach. It was a response I had never in my wildest thoughts expected. Whilst I was at the cashier's desk paying for the artworks — she said to a mutual friend, "that's the last time I'll stand aside at an auction for him"! (He told me later).

I was very puzzled by her attitude. Does one have to ask permission to wish someone well? It's a very normal human response when someone is suffering — for that suffering to end.

One could go on forever trying to understand her response but I guess there must be some sort of deep seated issue within her soul which I have no way of knowing about. Lesson learned. Just as treasure should be dug at midnight and not a word spoken — one has to apply that dictum to many other aspects of life. I guess we have to wait until we are asked for help if we wish to communicate as equals. If our desire to help happens to be rejected —then just send our love and ask Christ — or whoever one is connected to in deference — to help on our behalf.

So many times in my life I have had my helping hand accepted to my face but behind my back I have been ridiculed and laughed at. Nevertheless all people are our brothers and sisters and if one — even a Hitler or a Stalin — is unredeemed then part of us is also incomplete.

These destroyers of worlds are, in fact, I feel extensions of the base aspects of our own souls.

As I think I have already stated: "Free will is a two-edged sword indeed."

CHAPTER SIX

Dreams are amazing events in one's life — if we are 'awake' enough in our souls to appreciate the guidance they give us. Some are — or seem to be — very odd affairs and others can be very literal indeed.

There were two, not far apart, in 1990 which were, in fact, direct communications —one from a dead woman and one from a living woman. The first one involved a friend's home I had not visited for possibly thirty years — nor had I spoken to him for nearly that length of time. The first dream is as follows:

I knocked on the door and his mother (unbeknown to me, dead for several years) answered the door. She said, "You have been long enough getting in touch." I replied, "well, with a name like Smith, I had forgotten where you lived and there are so many in the phone book!" She replied, "that's OK, come in, Brian and his wife are here from the UK. They are out the back."

Then I awoke.

That morning I spent ages going through the phone book phoning Smiths who lived in the area. All in vain until I found one; and I recognised the name of the street. When I phoned, Brian's father answered and said the exact words his mother had said, adding "come on over. Brian and his wife are here from the UK for the holidays. They're out the back now." I did and was able to renew a friendship going back to kindergarten.

The other was, again, almost identical words as in the dream, etc. I heard the voice of my friend's mother saying, "you should get in touch with Alan—he is just fading away."

I remembered the suburb where he lived. He had inherited his uncle's home over thirty or more years ago. He worked for another airline when I worked for BOAC all those years before. We had not spoken for at least twenty plus years. I phoned his number and after asking how he was, he replied, "oh I'm just fading away!"

After a little bit of conversation he said, "oh, I have been meaning to get in touch with you as we have a mutual friend in San Francisco whom you have known since the 1960's and he visited you when you lived in Mosman but when you moved (he had moved from New York at the same time) both of you losing addresses." He gave me Thomas's phone number which I duly rang and we were able to pick up where we left off.

So both dreams had almost identical words spoken in the dream and in our reality. Both connections continued for many years until their deaths took them from this realm.

I feel there was some karmic connection in both cases and perhaps closure was required from one or both of us. It may have been only a few words spoken which were needed to alter my or their road in this life.

If we all had access to the Akashic records life could be very much simpler. Of course having said that — it would probably only open another Pandora's Box of challenges for us. Sometimes it is best not to know too much or we could be lulled into a state of despair or inertia.

Just prior to these events I was visiting my dear friend Murray at the Hospice in Darlinghurst. He had been ill for six years and had always said to me, "I will only live to my early forties." He often said that over the twenty plus years that I knew him. He had just turned 43. Some people just know things deep inside of themselves.

Years earlier another friend had asked a very fine psychic friend — who were Richard and Murray in past lives? He immediately replied that they were monks in Eleventh Century Europe and one had saved the other from drowning.

Getting back to that Sunday afternoon of October 1989, I was sitting next to him chatting about work etc, when I heard myself saying, "Oh Murray — your mother is here. She is standing at the end of the bed."

It was more felt than seen, but I was very sure as her image appeared to me mid- sentence about something completely different. I was always careful to talk only about happy, positive events.

He immediately said "I don't want to die."

I replied "She is here because she loves you so very much and only wants to help you." After another hour or so one could sense a complete change in his attitude. He seemed so much at peace and was almost cheery as I left.

I said to the nurse as I left, "Murray will be gone by Friday." "Oh no," she said "he is so positive and a real fighter. I know he was in awful pain from the cancer but he never complained."

I had phoned his father the week before to come up from Tasmania, but the doctor in charge of the hospice always gave him the opposite information, saying Murray was fine, etc. I phoned him again that night and, again, I was negated by the doctor's advice. By Wednesday, however, she had reversed her thinking and phoned him to come.

There was an airline strike on at the time so getting a flight was very difficult. On Thursday evening about 10.30, I received a call from his father at the hospice saying they had chartered a plane to Melbourne but could not get to Sydney until 11 am on Friday.

I went into Murray's room where the doctor was monitoring him. I told Murray he had to hang on until 11 am Friday as his father and brother were on their way. The doctor said, "He will not hear you — he is in a very deep coma."

I went home to bed and the following morning at 4.30, Murray's voice woke me, shouting my name, "Richard". It was as though he was on the top of one mountain and I on another. I sat up and said out loud. "Murray — how did you get here — it's all locked up?"

Out of the corner of my eye I saw a penny glow in the dark. I knew he had died and was paying the boatman to cross the river Styx.

I knew the nurse would phone me soon and sure enough five minutes later the phone rang with the news. He had died at 4.30 am.

At 5.15 am I drove to the hospice and sat with him for two hours, reminiscing about all our adventures over the last twenty-one years. He lay as asleep and I expected he would turn to me to say, "Oh, for goodness sakes, let me rest!" The nurse told me as I was leaving that Murray had awoken out of his coma at 4 am and she had said,

"Murray—do you want some morphine?" He replied —"No, I want to be awake when my father comes at 11 am."

So he had heard me despite the doctor's denial.

Over the next forty-eight hours one could feel the space he had occupied whilst in his physical body. He was often standing nearby as we spoke to his relations and friends. Gradually the space closed up and he had begun his journey home.

A few months later I dreamt I met him in a most beautiful valley. He looked so well. I said, "Murray — you look so young and fit." He replied, "I'm gradually putting myself back together again."

I asked him — "Have you met anyone you knew whilst on earth?" He replied, "Oh yes—people I knew well who have crossed over. I can talk with them and they are very clear. Others whom I knew — but not well — I can see, but there is very little communication. People who I had heard of — or didn't know — I can feel they are present, but they are mere shadows."

As he was saying this, a young woman, whom I knew in the dream, but had forgotten since, rushed up to him and flung her arms around him. He greeted her warmly and they spoke for a minute or so.

Then she left.

As we walked along I said to him, "What's it like over the other side?" He said, "I can't tell you too much but there are lots of willow trees!"

I said, "Willow trees?"

He said, "Yes — but I have to go now." Then, as we walked, he gradually evaporated from my sight.

Telling a friend of the dream, he said he had a book on myths and legends, perhaps the willow trees may be of some significance. A few days later he brought the book over. There was a page on the 'Weeping Willow Tree'. In many cultures it was the symbol of death and mourning.

One of the dreams a few months later was very interesting. Murray had featured in several dreams which I have neglected to write down.

In this dream he had knocked on my door and when I opened it I said, "Murray, what are you doing here?" He said, "I'm starving — give me something to eat." I replied, "But you're dead — you don't need food anymore." He repeated his request for food. We went to the kitchen where I made two poached eggs for him. As he sat down to eat, again there was a knock at the door. Upon opening, I was greeted by some friends calling by unannounced. I told them Murray was in the kitchen. They said, "Don't be ridiculous." When we entered the kitchen Murray was gone but on the plate were two broken egg shells. Perhaps a sign that life goes on and from the egg comes new forms of life — either on this plane or, perhaps, others.

Just before he died he told a mutual friend he wished he had listened to me more about the afterlife as he was fearful as to what was in store.

Also, I feel the dead are in need of spiritual food that we can give them by remembering them with loving thoughts. The ancient Egyptians always painted the tombs with pictures of food laid out ready to be eaten — plus real food placed in urns, etc, for the souls on their journey.

Many cultures still remember the dead — holding feast days in their memory.

I do feel all the people we meet in a lifetime — all have had some sort of connection with us in a past life.

Also I feel this plane is the one where we can, on balance, advance and balance our karma.

If we can open our third eye whilst in a physical body — we are at a great advantage when we cross over. We almost have prior information as to what is in store on that phase of our journey.

At the time of Christ's death, the veil of the temple was torn asunder. It symbolised change for the whole of humanity.

Prior to Christ's incarnation all occult initiation was tightly controlled by the priesthood and initiates. Christ opened the door for all to gain entrance into the spiritual world through their own efforts.

Often it is said — when the student is ready the teacher will come. Every day of our lives there are teachers on many levels all around us. It is just a matter of becoming awake to these synchronistic signs and events

Christ also said, "Let the dead bury the dead."

Initiates always say —"I came to life at that moment. I was dead in spirit before I awoke." As I mentioned earlier, so many people are controlled by their environmental conditioning and that sheer joy of being alive when they were young has been lulled to sleep. The word 'clairvoyant' only means 'clear sightedness'. All of us are forever waking up, emerging from the mist of our past even though we may not be aware of it happening.

All part of our journey to see life as it truly is for us at our particular railway platform as we hop from train to train, trying to reach that unfathomable goal or destination.

CHAPTER SEVEN

My first flat after I left home in 1964 was a small bed sitter in Neutral Bay. It had only been constructed a couple of years prior to my tenancy.

I made the furniture and bought some I could not make. The works of Salvador Dali and El Greco were fascinating to me at the time. I had purchased reproductions of 'Storm over Toledo' and two of Dali's religious images.

When one looks back one wonders how one was able to afford such luxuries. The prints cost ten guineas each with a similar cost for framing. I was only earning eleven pounds a week then! The furniture I made for friends would have helped me earn this extra cash, no doubt.

Anyway I furnished the flat as best I could and as I may have already said, the skin problems which I had endured for over five years disappeared within two weeks. (No stress.)

The odd thing was — although I loved having my own abode for the first time ever, it was still not a home with my stamp on it. The atmosphere was cold and austere.

One evening, after I had been there for about five months, I was watching television — in the days before remote controls. I got up to change to one of the three channels broadcasting then and as I did a strange thing happened.

In an instant I felt myself expand in an astral sense to every corner of the room and at the same time 'heard' myself saying in a deep voice —"my aura now pervades this space." In another instant I was back inside of my own self once more. It gave me quite a shock but deep down I thought something just happened that needed to be done.

A few months later I learnt the wife of the previous tenant had committed suicide due to post-natal depression. Her soul being must have still been attached to the flat. Somehow my 'higher self' was aware of all this and did a cleansing! Afterwards people used to remark how cosy and inviting my apartment was.

I had made it my own.

However, after I left the Bank of NSW to join BOAC as their accountant in Sydney in 1966, I had to give it up as my salary just did not allow for travel away for any length of time and also pay the rent as well.

I moved four times in the next two years before I found a wonderful flat on the waterfront at North Sydney. Having a flat mate halved the rent, still only similar to that paid in 1964, but it allowed me to take a trip to New York in 1968 for my Christmas holidays. I stayed with a friend whom I met in Europe the previous year and enjoyed the wonderful cultural life of that City.

The Lincoln Centre had only recently been completed and although the temperature was always in the minus on the scale I was able to buy a ticket the following Saturday for Wagner's 'Mastersingers'. After purchasing, I walked to Philharmonic Hall, looking at the programs.

An old lady approached me and said, "would you like to attend the concert this afternoon? My friend is at the dentist and cannot come. If I give back her ticket to the box office when it is sold, the money goes to the musicians' benevolent fund. If not sold, it's just wasted." I readily agreed and offered to pay. "Oh no", she said, "my treat. Where are you from?" When I told her, she took me to the box office and introduced me to the clerk. "This young man," she said, "is all the way from Sydney, Australia and he will be coming in Maureen's place this afternoon." Later the box office clerk came up to me and told me my benefactor never missed a concert on a Friday since the Hall was opened and was a major donor to the arts in New York.

I rushed home to West 78th Street to change and was able to buy a bunch of roses for her two seconds before the doors closed.

It was a wonderful concert, conducted by Carlo Maria Giulini and the feature artist was the pianist, Rudolf Firkusny.

At the end of the concert my patron introduced me to another friend who promptly gave me two tickets for the following day's matinee performance of 'La Sonnambula' starring Joan Sutherland.

That evening I said to my host, "We are going to the opera tomorrow"—and recounted my good fortune for the day. His reply was "Goddammit — all that

happens to me in this town is I get kicked in the backside and you arrive and are promptly given hundreds of dollars worth of tickets!"

We both laughed at the vagaries of fate and next day experienced 'Our Joan' at her prime.

Again, when one thinks about it, what are the chances of being in that place at that exact moment in time for all that abundance to just materialize out of thin air?

These synchronistic events always tell me I am in the right lane going in the right direction on life's highway. It may be not the ideal road but it is one that harmonises with the karma I have to experience during this lifetime.

CHAPTER EIGHT

My Grandmother, on my father's side of the family, passed away in 1964.

According to family history, she was a descendant from the George Stephenson family. A remarkable woman who never criticized anyone or spoke ill of them. She played the piano, wrote poetry and short stories. She also had ten children in a tiny house built at the turn of the twentieth century by my grandfather who was a supervisor at North Sydney Council.

When I was young we only visited their home at Christmas and Easter so I never really got to know them until I was in my teens and would play hooky on sports day at high school.

Marched to North Sydney oval for rugby — which was not my cup of tea at all — I would linger back until I was last in the line and at the appropriate time slip behind a tree as they were marched off down the hill. I would then go to my grandparent's home for lunch and spend the afternoon sitting on the veranda listening to all their life adventures.

Grandma had a friend called Mary. She was always at the house in those years as a frequent visitor and guest.

One Easter when our family were visiting, Mary took me aside and whispered, "Don't tell anyone"—and handed me a ten shilling note. As an eight year old, no one had ever given me a ten shilling note. She said "spend it at the Easter Show." I thought Mary was an angel sent from the heavens and I loved her so much.

When I was about twelve or thirteen, I had a revelation. Mary was black! I had never seen the colour of her skin before! She was as black as coal — born in Torres Straight Islands. I had only ever seen a beautiful spirit — never the skin she was wearing.

It is only the conditioning we receive in our lives that determine our 'prejudices', etc. One can see how hatreds of other religions and social backgrounds are passed down through generations.

As I said in the beginning — the sins of the fathers are passed on and on and on until one day someone in that chain 'wakes up' and thinks for themselves.

Mary was a trained nurse who worked as a domestic help in a grand home down the road from Grandma. In the mid nineteen thirties, Grandma noticed her sitting on the low wall in front of the home each Thursday afternoon. Grandma asked her why and she replied, "It's my day off." Grandma said, "Don't sit there, come up to my house and we can chat" which they did for nearly thirty years and only ended with Grandma's death in 1964. Grandpa had died the previous year. Gran never saw anything negative in anyone and even in my father's case she would say to his siblings, "don't disturb Neil, he's just different."

Indeed, his siblings were all the most kind, gentle folk one could ever hope to meet in this world.

CHAPTER NINE

I feel some of our dreams are, in fact, fragmented memories of what our 'finer bodies' do whilst our physical body is asleep.

This particular dream occurred a few times from 1970 on. Each time some of the main occurrences happened a couple of times and minor details were a little different.

Perhaps I was interacting with some people trapped in a purgatory of their own making. People who had died so quickly, they were unaware they had, in fact, passed over. Very often these people have never given a minute's thought to anything other than their day to day existence on Earth. They have no comprehension of the dimension they now inhabit and often are trapped there — sometimes for centuries.

There are always beings waiting to help them — but they cannot interfere unless they are asked by the lost souls.

The dream began in a park where the trees had died — but still looked to be alive. I was sitting on a park bench and a branch fell from a tree near me. It gave me a great shock as it almost exploded as it hit the ground, shattering like glass. There were no other people around at all. Moments later I found myself in a boat with a woman I knew whom I am sure would have passed over by then. She was a mutual friend of an Australian girl I knew and a man born in Shanghai as was the woman also. Both were of European descent.

Nancy (her name) took me from the mooring and we walked to a beautiful 1930's home —wonderfully preserved. One large room had very high ceilings; all lined in plywood veneer, moulded and shaped. A sloping mezzanine floor overhung a kitchen and bathroom. Almost a stage setting. Everything beyond the house appeared deserted and there were no cars. I asked how often the buses ran. No answer, I seem to remember.

I made some coffee and was thinking how delicious it was when I spilt some on Nancy's dress. She said, "don't worry, it won't stain—it's clear." To my consternation it was, indeed, clear. In another version of the dream she said that the scientists make everything, now, from formulas and there was no need to grow anything. She continued "it's all manufactured in giant factories." It was incredible how tasty the coffee was.

The walls were decorated in Art Deco Murals, depicting mushroom houses and flowers with coloured lights in them. One wall had millions of snails on it. I enquired as to whether she was not worried about dampness. Nancy replied that she was not worried at all and that everything just fixed itself.

Then a lot of people began to arrive. Some of us sat at a table for a meal. A small girl in a white frilly dress of Edwardian design joined us.

An inner voice said to me, "all is not as it seems. These people are dead and do not know it." Something made me look into the mirror on the wall behind me to test if they had any reflection. There was none. Where the little girl was sitting the mirror depicted an ant-like metallic creature — whitish-grey with large black eyes.

Turning back to the table — everything was as before.

More people arrived. One young man placed a small oblong shaped object against my ear. It made a buzzing sound. Again, something inside me warned me not to listen to it or I could become like them.

That is — a sort of living dead.

I grabbed him and after much struggle was able to place the object against his ear. No one attempted to help him and the room was full of people by now. He screamed and then collapsed on the floor. Half of his insides seemed to just disappear. He became as light as a feather as I carried his sack like body to another room and cleared a space on a chair, where I placed him. I returned to the main room.

One of the excited crowd said "now we can make the movie ourselves — the one they said we could not make."

In an instant all these misshapen — and some downright ugly — people were performing in a Busby Berkeley type spectacular. One of them glared at me with a look full of hate. I decided to leave but thought I would come back later and look through the window.

They began an amazing dance sequence. Again I was thinking about what seemed to be a non-existent bus service.

I watched black ants running backwards and forwards, each carrying a grain of cooked rice! I reflected on the people inside the house and wondered why did they not know they were dead.

Perhaps they had died so suddenly or frightfully that they, in fact, had left their bodies seconds prior to its death. I have heard that people who have been murdered in the most horrendous way have told mediums they had done that spontaneously — thus avoiding those final moments.

As I began to wake up a thought came to me. I had glimpsed a realm associated with Hollywood and perhaps a neutron bomb had been detonated — destroying all forms of life — reducing living plants and people to a crystalline structure — but leaving all buildings intact.

As I said — this dream occurred two or three times around that time in my life. Perhaps what I remember has been somewhat garbled a bit by my inability to recall it all. I wrote down at the time what I remembered. The metallic like creature could easily have been a sort of inter-dimensional being and the small vibrating box some sort of control device.

No doubt many devices and seemingly real worlds are created by the thoughts and actions of the inhabitants.

In many cultures, days are set aside to pray and think of the dead. It harkens back to those nights when I was very young and I could see all these trapped souls in my room. Perhaps they felt, somehow, I could help them in some way.

POSTSCRIPT

I feel the dead are aghast at how quickly they are forgotten in this time of instant gratification. They gather around us in our quiet moments, hoping for some, or even longing for spiritual nourishment. A food prepared by our loving thoughts and worthy compassionate deeds.

Alas, they find the table bare.

On this plane, nature provides for us in abundance. A fruit tree gives us far more than one person can eat and yet when it comes to feeding the departed we are very mean.

It is food for the soul these spirits crave — food not for ingestion but some food created by our loving, clear, spiritual thoughts and deeds.

If we have lived a life of solitude and selfishness that loneliness continues into the spirit realms.

All the links, associations — good and bad deeds — and thoughts continue. As below — so above (and vice-versa).

Remembering our loved ones for the rest of our lives is the greatest gift we can give to them. Not in a sorrowful way but including them in our daily lives — even remarking — "Oh my goodness—what do you think about that—(so and so)?" Or—"I hope you were not around when I did (such and such). How could I have been so stupid?" Laugh with them and share your life. When alone, talk out loud to them. They were part of your world once and no doubt will be in the future.

Visualize their faces and in your mind's eye surround them with white light.

There is no need to be thought of as clinging to the past. Just find your own way that feels right for you.

If you discuss these things with friends — I am afraid the common response will be to ridicule or demean. Don't cast your pearls before swine!

CHAPTER TEN

Revelations can happen in the most unlikely places. During my first trip to London in 1966 I was staying at a small hotel — not paying a lot for the room whilst a travelling companion (the man whose mother I mentioned in a dream had told me to get in touch with) was staying in a Grand Hotel near Marble Arch.

One morning I was sitting in the lobby awaiting his arrival in the lift when two very tall, stout, late middle aged women strode past me. I think I discerned an American accent as they spoke. Their attire could have come straight from the nineteen twenties-thirties.

Not taking much notice, I nearly fell off my chair when I 'saw' a long line of animal forms slowly walking behind them. There were cows, chickens, ducks, geese, what looked like a bison and, even a crocodile! Those are some of the slaughtered animal forms that had been dissected, butchered, cooked and carved up for these two women to consume.

They were indeed the walking graveyard of these wondrous creatures.

What a world we have created!

And yet, should I judge them? I think not as I am far from perfect and who knows, consuming animals and animal products may all be part of the evolving chain of life.

If one gives up eating these sentient beings and yet still lusts after the taste and smells of the cooked animal, then perhaps they are not ready to embark on the journey. As I often observe, so many people just live for their taste buds. Forever searching for that new taste sensation.

CHAPTER ELEVEN

Back in 1986 a very dear friend died in the street on his way to see me.

He was a great walker and when young had walked throughout Europe in the 1920's and thirties. He was very much involved with the Christian Community Church. A true seeker of spiritual values. Years earlier I predicted he would die in the street. In fact it was in front of our favourite restaurant in Sydney, Sandro's Italian Restaurant in William Street, Kings Cross. For years we had gone there for their fresh food — beautifully, simply cooked by his two Italian women chefs who had been with him for years. I first went there in 1967.

I had told my friend who died not to come for dinner that Sunday night as I would be flat out getting gallery opening invitations labelled and posted. I was running behind schedule.

On Sunday at about 2.30 pm, I walked to Potts Point Post Office with about a third of the invites and popped them in the posting bins.

I then started to walk to Macleay Regis where he lived—thinking we would have a cup of tea. I got nearly to the door and thought, no; I'll never get all the work done if I take time off now; so I turned around and walked back to Woolloomooloo.

Next day his nephew phoned me asking had I seen Alfred. I said I hadn't and told him about our cancellation of Sunday night's dinner at my place.

The following day his body was found at the morgue. He had died of a heart attack outside Sandro's Restaurant. He was 83. His wallet was missing, hence the lack of identification until the Tuesday, by his nephew. In his will, he had left the flat to his nephew, along with his wonderful collection of bronzes.

Six months later a friend of many years told me he had bought a flat on the top floor of Sandro's Building and in due course I was invited to dinner to inspect their transformation from an early Depression dump into a very comfortable apartment. Twelve months later my friend phoned to say he had sold it for an excellent price and was moving.

Before he could tell me where, I said, "Macleay Regis?" He said "Yes, how did you know?" I said "Sixth floor?" He replied, "Yes". I indicated the flat number. He again said, "How did you know?" I replied, "Alfred organised it from the other side, I am sure, so I can, one more time sit in his former home with him whilst I have a meal with you!" Which I did and, felt his presence very strongly. We did, indeed, have a unique friendship. He was a man of great spirituality.

When Sandro closed his restaurant and returned to Italy we stayed in touch for several years by correspondence.

I think the events I have described go far beyond mere coincidence.

All my life I have observed incidents that seemed to unfold into other events — sometimes I have thought, why have I gone down this avenue? It seems like a horrible dead end. Then it turned out later on — if I had not made these seeming mistakes the subsequent rewards would never have occurred.

The power of observation is critical in awakening inner intuition and higher thought. One uses one's mind to solve these seemingly ordinary and sometimes boring events which fill most of our lives.

There is something to be learnt from every experience once you learn to observe. Also, I have found if you confide in people, most will dismiss you as a crank or worse. Best to keep one's thoughts close to the chest and talk only of those things when you discover a kindred spirit.

A few years ago, I was reading a book which showed a photo of Foulis Castle near Inverness, Scotland; the home of the Munro Clan. That was the place where my mum's mum worked as lady in waiting to Lady Violet Munro in the early part of the twentieth century.

I said out loud, "Gran I have at last seen a picture of the castle you worked in and told me so much about when I was young. If you can hear me Gran—give me a sign tomorrow."

The next evening my cousin Bruce phoned me. He is the son of mum's brother. It was the first time I had spoken to Bruce in over fifty years. The last time was at Gran's funeral.

It was not the day before that I had asked Gran for a sign — nor the day after — it was exactly on the day I wanted.

Again — beyond — way beyond chance.

CHAPTER TWELVE

Some dreams appear out of the blue and are extremely bizarre, to say the least. Tell six different people skilled in dream interpretation and one will get six different scenarios.

In the early 1990's I experienced several annoying dreams that resonated in my mind for a very long time. One of them which I will include later in this book is so (to me) amazing; I feel it could be developed into a short story on its own.

Often in myth and literature up until our present time it has been shown redemption and love go hand in hand. Most of Wagner's music dramas have that quality. The dream I mentioned was an amazing example of the process.

The following one is, I am sure, open to all sorts of interpretation. I will let it speak for itself.

Four bodies had been laid out — side by side. There were no coffins. All were wearing the clothes they had died in. There were no signs of injury to any of the bodies and somehow I knew that each had died only a short time before. A cat — a pet belonging to one of the deceased — also dead — was placed next to his mistress.

A crowd of on-lookers stood a few metres away. I got a feeling they were afraid of what they were seeing and there was much excited talk amongst them. They also seemed to know how they had died.

The tomb in this ancient cemetery was a traditional one from the time of Christ. It was a small cave with a huge stone slab leaning next to the entrance.

A woman whom I knew (in the dream) came very happily up to the bodies and looked them over. Her demeanour seemed to be very upsetting to the spectators as there was much muttering amongst them.

Turning to me she said, "Oh I can easily bring them back to life." Then, as she spoke, she produced a small phial of clear liquid which she sprinkled on to the chest of each corpse including the cat.

It was the first to spring back to life — which is certainly what it did. Jumping up it shook itself violently and seemed very disturbed — immediately taking off in the opposite direction of the crowd at great speed.

A young woman — dressed in a simple smock dress of very coarse weave started to rise, a look of extreme anger on her face. As soon as she was on her feet she demanded to know who was responsible for bringing her back to life.

My companion proudly stated that she was the one who performed this miraculous deed. Her reward from the woman resurrected was, "How dare you!" By this time the crowd were at fever pitch — hurling abuse at this woman who had the audacity to play a god.

Within a few seconds the three other corpses — all men — were once again vital living beings. They did not seem to be as agitated as the young woman had been.

They just stood there in a very dazed state not seeming to know who they were or where they were.

I viewed this drama with a mixture of apprehension and wonder. Turning to this 'Priestess' with the power of life over death, I asked her, "Do you think we should bring back the dead?"

Her reply — again full of confidence and obvious sincerity was "Sixteen years ago, the girl in this photo was killed in an accident. I revived her.

Now look at the list of achievements she has made during those sixteen years. She had a mission to complete—I helped her do it."

"What if the person's time is up and you bring them back when they should not be?" I asked.

"They will die once more and not long after I have revived them. What is the difference between my work and a high tech hospital where people are kept alive by machines or are revived after the collapse of vital organs — where people receive new hearts, lungs or kidneys? We are all playing God now."

With those words the scene receded and I sank into a revere — half awake, half asleep. The only 'thing' we can take from this world is experience — not knowledge as knowledge exists. All we do is discover it, adapt it and mould it to suit our needs — but the experience of life on this physical plane is unique. Perhaps the gods — and the angels might envy us because every time we experience an event it is unique in the universe — in time, space and other dimensions, also. Some experiences may seem similar to those of other people — but they are not the same, as our lives will colour it and adapt to it to make it our own. All as individual as our fingerprint.

Perhaps the onlookers represented the old view that we should not tamper with nature. But we must — for if we are to become gods ourselves we must 'know' both sides of the equation. The peak of the highest mountain against the depth of the lowest valley. The greater the light against the deeper darker shadow.

Only then will we become truly free — free of the gods who are our co-creators and, hopefully, all tempered by universal love.

We cannot know what the future of mankind is — but whatever it is, it is the greatest adventure we can ever comprehend. It will never end because there is no beginning or ending — just infinite possibility.

With these words the 'dream' faded and I was once more myself with all my faults and desires that truly make me who I am.

CHAPTER THIRTEEN

Jean — a Sydney writer, journalist and critic — died on Anzac Day 1992 at her home in North Queensland. A close, dear friend of twenty plus years, she was in her mid- sixties. I think she died more from loneliness than what was written on the doctor's death certificate.

In this dream of July 1993 — just over a year after she died — I was walking with another friend towards her old home in Sydney. A tube made of metal — which I was carrying was filled with the freshest, cleanest and sweetest water I had ever tasted. I discovered that however much I drank, it would refill immediately. All I had to do was run my hand over the top of it and it was as if it was coming from a tap. Upon reaching Jean's house I was met by her at the door, sadly looking as unwell as she was at the time of her death.

I asked her for an empty glass and by simply passing my hand over it — it was full of the same strange water. Jean drank the water and immediately became her youthful self once more — even a little taller than she had been in those last years.

She had been a champion swimmer when young and had led an adventurous life exploring the Pacific islands and many countries abroad.

Her home was in a very sad state of repair; paint was peeling off everything.

When I waved my hand over the walls the old paint would fall away, revealing beautiful paint underneath made up of layers of several colours; very hard to describe.

When I finished 'repainting' the house, I turned my attention to the furniture. Again waving my hand over it, it seemed to come to life — like it was breathing! Some pieces would puff up, roll from side to side as the old varnish or finish gave way to a glorious piece of furniture.

Jean had been a great collector of art and antiques all her life in Sydney.

One piece of furniture obviously had a mind of its own; a desk which swelled up much bigger than it was and then disappeared under an antique rug.

It created a huge mound in the middle of the room. I tried in vain to coax it out again, to no avail. I decided in my mind it just had to go. Upon my command it disappeared.

I said to Jean, I was sorry she had lost her desk but she replied, "Don't worry I am just so happy to be well once more." Strangely she seemed even taller than she had been a little while ago. There the dream ended.

(Time is very difficult to gauge in dreams.)

Only a month before this dream I had been on holiday on Magnetic Island at a friend's home. The house—a typical Queenslander—on stilts, had been brought from the mainland in bits and reassembled there.

Out of the corner of my eye I would often see a woman standing in the front room of the house. Later I wondered if it was Jean, asking for help.

Upon waking from this dream I had a feeling something very positive had been accomplished.

Jean had helped me throughout the years I knew her — often writing excellent articles about my gallery in the National newspaper she worked for. She had also named me co-executor in her will. A very kind, generous woman who, sadly, had a very lonely existence. Her marriages did not last and some so-called 'friends' seemed to have taken advantage of her.

From what I have learned over the years it appears we reconstruct our world as we have it now, in the hereafter. Hence the broken body and house in great disrepair.

Jean must have asked for help as she realized her new state of being and seemed unable to rectify it herself.

The water would symbolise, I feel, the life blood of all living beings from plants to animals, to us.

Also, our minds having created this duplicate realm can also change it — once we discover we have that ability.

Jean was born in North Queensland and died there, having moved to be near her former husband who, unfortunately, was not of the same mind.

As below — so above. So many people think it's going to be all sweetness and light when we cross over; but unless we spend some time of our lives thinking about spiritual matters, we stay very connected to this physical realm.

CHAPTER FOURTEEN

As a child I had loved growing plants and by the age of eight or nine had a thriving vegetable patch. I'm ashamed to say I would often 'borrow' small plants from nature strips outside neighbours' homes — making sure there was as little evidence as possible that a plant had been 'relocated'. Looking back I often wonder if the owners of the property saw me and what thoughts went through their minds. I was never caught in the act (luckily) and whenever I did meet up with any of the owners at funerals, in later years, all were very kind and friendly.

On the other hand my father would look at my thriving garden and say, "if you leave that shovel out, I will belt you!" Talk about encouraging a child!!

The local variety store in the shopping centre sold plants in old jam tins at reasonable prices. (There were no plastic throw away containers then.)

For some reason I was especially fond of pencil pines and when I saw one there — very, very tiny for two shillings — I managed to rake up the funds to buy it. Proudly showing it to my mother I determined the best place for it was next to the front gate. It was planted that afternoon.

A few days later, my father must have spied it there (it was very small). He announced at the dinner table — his favourite venue to harass and terrify everyone — that the plant had to go. My reaction was swift. "It's staying there." I said. He replied, "I'll pull it out then." "All right" I said, "if you do — whilst you're at work tomorrow I'll pull out all of your plants that I can." Of course, he exploded — causing the usual huge row, with my mother taking to her bed with a migraine.

We were never allowed to enjoy a meal in that house. Every meal was an ordeal — no one was allowed to laugh or even talk without his thundering on and on. Horrible.

His drinking only made him worse. He was unable to love and cherish his three daughters and two sons. I told him in later years he was well balanced — having a chip on each shoulder.

Their marriage — when one reads the letters they sent to each other prior to the wedding are happy and very normal. It seems something happened to him in his late thirties and from being almost a puritan, he morphed into the 'horror' he became. (Must have been 'something nasty in the wood shed' ha ha).

He knew if I said I would do something, I would do it. Once before he had hurled a pot plant I had placed on the front porch and it smashed into bits. I had said to him that two could be childish and picked up one of his prize stag horn ferns and did the same. This led to a huge verbal clash and a chase — so loud the neighbours came out to tell him to desist and be thankful he had such fine children. Of course if he was not feuding with them himself he was running them down behind their backs.

Over the years the pencil pine grew and grew very happily in its piece of earth. In fact it became a landmark in the district. People would tell friends to get off the bus at the house with the large pencil pine at the gate.

In 1968 they sold the house. The neighbours also decided to sell — to developers.

Our block was very large with huge trees at the rear. All were levelled — not a blade of grass remained. However, the pencil pine did remain.

Fast forward to Anzac Day, 1995. My father died in hospital. He was 86. Mum had died six years earlier.

Driving to his house in Baulkham Hills to sort things out, I drove by our old home. The pencil pine had gone. My brother told me it was removed that day by the body corporate of the flats!

Synchronicity at work once more. The chances of it going the day he died are amazing. So he finally got his way!

Over the years I had always looked out for it as I drove by and often it was a talking point with my siblings. I never discussed it with my parents.

It may be that it was a thorn in my father's side that my tiny little tree was all that had survived the massacre of our home and land. One never knows.

Years later a dear friend who is clairvoyant told me my mother and her mother were nearby and my mum was so happy to see me — calling me by her favourite shortening of my name. My friend said, "I can't see your father. Oh, there he is, coming out of a shed and waving." I remarked that he had spent his life pottering in his shed. He had, in fact, been a man of great talent.

Anything he put his hand to turned out to be the very very best. I used to joke, "here he is—the Third Reich Building Company. Everything guaranteed to last a thousand years!" "Anyway," he said, "let bygones be bygones." Again—he was still trapped in his own thought world but no doubt had been able to review his life and it was his way of saying sorry. When I had scattered his ashes at Bundeena where he had built a holiday shack in the 1930's I spent an hour or so 'talking' with him about our relationship. Taking my own advice I had given to that woman in David Jones all those years ago I had let go of all the trauma of a long time ago and asked his forgiveness as I wished to forgive him also.

My siblings had wanted to be there but as the years went on after his cremation I told them I would do the deed on my own and they were happy with that.

His ashes were cast from the rock where he used to catch fish.

His life had come full circle.

CHAPTER FIFTEEN

It has been reported that on his deathbed Alexander the Great made three requests:
· The finest doctors in the land should carry his coffin.
· All his worldly wealth his gold money gems etc be strewn either side of the avenue to his burial site.
· The last request — that his hands be exposed outside of his coffin for everyone to see.

Asked why he made such odd requests he explained as follows:
"When the people see the finest doctors in the world carrying my coffin they will know —when death's time has come — all their efforts to prolong life will be in vain.
By sharing my wealth with those who are left behind they will know the wealth I acquired on Earth remains on Earth.
By exposing my hands to the populace they will understand we come into this world empty handed and leave empty handed.
Our most valuable treasure, time has been exhausted.
Time cannot be recreated. It is a very limited, precious possession. We can create more wealth should we lose it. We cannot recreate more time once it has gone."

When we give of our time, it is gone forever. Our life and time are one.

There is also another way of looking at time — if it is a phenomenon of this realm alone and only exists on this level of vibration. Perhaps we live in a multi-dimensional universe where past present and future are all one! Everything we ever were — are or will be — is happening at once! A concept very hard to assimilate even by the most advanced intelligence, I feel. Perhaps there is no beginning or end. Concepts not for the faint hearted — indeed.

Looking back—everyone I know who is in my age group all say —"Where did our lifetime go?" It is indeed just the blink of an eye. One sometimes wonders — why do men make war on each other? Unless one wipes out the defeated entirely — those who remain usually triumph later on. All is so ephemeral — so fleeting — but of course we can only come to these conclusions through the doing — through the deed itself. Through learning the hard way.

People know some foods — drugs — habits etc are bad for one but until they taste the consequences of their actions — they do not learn — unfortunately sometimes far too late.

So, perhaps, it is all in the 'deed'. Words can become hollow until one actually has the real time/space related experience — which is a result of our thinking or even lack of. Then the deed resonates to our very soul and changes us in a way all the thinking in the world will not.

Synchronicity, I feel, is also a vital component of our lives. It has guided me through many periods of my life. Often it is upon reflection we see a pattern emerge — again the power of observation.

Little things like walking the dog or taking another route on our journey where we meet people who are or can become important in our lives. What appears to be a chance encounter could in reality be a guiding hand.

So many times I have been in the 'right' place at the 'right' time. Like standing in a line waiting for a ticket for a concert — people have approached me so many times throughout my life in many countries all over the world and offered a free seat or even years ago at Heathrow

Airport where there had been a strike for several days of which I was unaware —arriving to find thousands of people desperate to get a flight.

I mentioned to the check-in clerk that if I could get to Rome, I could pick up a Lufthansa flight to Hong Kong then a connection to Sydney. No sooner had I found a place to sit and wait when the Captain of a BOAC flight to Tel Aviv approached me and offered me a seat in the cockpit. This was the 'jump seat', usually reserved for crew members to discuss items with the captain whilst in mid-flight. I was happy to sit upfront and accepted. Again it was being there just at that magic moment in time.

Several years ago I was visiting my doctor as I had suffered for about eight years with an autoimmune illness. I remarked how fit and well and younger he looked and he told me his wife was vegan — and he had become vegan as well. The change in his appearance was remarkable.

That morning upon returning home I found an email from a publisher in the US about two billionaires who had become vegan through viewing a DVD called 'EATING'. I said to myself, Ah-ha—synchronicity telling me something again. So I ordered the DVD.

The instant I viewed it my thoughts were clarified on so many issues that I resolved to eat only a plant-based diet from that day on.

It has been life enhancing on so many levels and of course there is nothing worse than the recently converted. I purchased many copies of the DVD through the local vegetarian society and off line and gave them to everyone I thought would benefit.

Sadly many (years later) I found out had not even bothered to watch it — others were indifferent and about a dozen or more have embraced this compassionate life style and are very happy they did.

Of course as we are free human beings who also have karmic lessons to unfold —perhaps people are not ready to take such a road just yet.

I had been vegetarian for a few years when young but travelling a lot and dining with friends (who went to a lot of trouble creating a special meal for me), I drifted away from the idealism I embraced at the time. Perhaps 'life changes' often happen when everything fits into the right energy field we have been creating for most of our lives.

Perhaps at a very deep level — perfect justice does rule the world even though it appears to be the very opposite.

Animals, insects, plants, minerals and we, ourselves, are all very much interdependent and connected on so many levels.

In the higher animals — that is those domesticated animals, such as the horse and the dog and, to some extent, the house cat — are all animals very close to man and even at the point of their evolution, on the cusp of becoming human. The love they give is possibly one of the purist forms I know. It is without any form of judgment and they seem to be able to forgive us no matter what.

A popular book such as 'Wizard of Oz' which is part of the American psyche has many levels of meaning. The author was a theosophist and despite his early business failings went on to write other American classics.

On one level one can discern the evolution of American libertarian principles. The 'Yellow Brick Road' represents the gold standard — Emerald City the greenback dollar, Dorothy's slippers (in the books they were silver), represented the pure silver dollar. A monetary system built on a firm foundation. Not like today with printing machines churning out notes twenty-four hours a day. See the DVD 'The Secret of Oz', directed by Bill Still (2009) www.secretofoz.com (highly recommended).

On another level one could say the straw man represents the plant kingdom wanting to think in its own individual ways. The tin man representing the mineral world, wanting to feel and the lion wanting courage. The animal kingdom wanting free will — to break free of its group soul — to individualise.

It follows the three most potent forces in this world: Thinking—feeling and willing.

There are so many classic tales given to humanity by enlightened beings which work upon us at deep levels — shaping our own ever expanding consciousness.

In the case of Richard Wagner, I know of many people who will not experience his music dramas because of what they perceive as a composer who had many flaws and anti-Semitic views. They are denying themselves a life enhancing/changing experience.

Again, judge the prophets by the great gifts they gave to humanity — not their feet of clay.

CHAPTER SIXTEEN

As I mentioned earlier — my correspondence with George Adamski led to my lifelong friendship with my science teacher from school and opened so many other doors for me.

Over the years I continued to study the phenomenon of UFO's and related material. Back in the 1970's I had what I thought to be dreams of being on board these craft over time.

As I was being given some acupuncture by a dear friend she remarked about two scarab shaped lumps on my stomach. She said, "What's this?" My immediate reaction — which upon reflection — I was surprised. I said, "Oh they are nothing to worry about. Ignore them." The fact was it was the first I knew of their existence, but was confident in myself they were of no concern whatsoever.

A month or so later she remarked that they had gone. During that time I had never bothered to even look, myself, if they were still there. Later I wondered why I had been so indifferent.

Could they have been a sort of tracking device—implanted by an alien culture? Were these 'dreams' not dreams at all—but memories of a very real experience?

I have read many books on the subject by dozens of authors over the course of my life. Many of them had experiences which — when talked about — left them open to ridicule. In academia any professor who took the subject seriously was almost kicked out of the system.

Science used to be, in days long gone, an avenue of open minded enquiry where all possibilities were looked at in an effort to find some truth. Not anymore. Dogma has infiltrated these hallowed halls of learning and enquiry and it has become the new orthodoxy.

However, in March 1994 I had a very real encounter with alien life. I was alone at my farm in southern NSW when I awoke at 3 am. It was as though car headlights had briefly lit up my room. My bed faced large French doors and I had a clear view of the sky as the shrubs were small and I could see far into the distance of State forest.

Silently 'sitting' about a mile or two up in the starry sky was a craft the size of a small town. It was enormous — circular — and from the underbelly there was what appeared to be airlocks where smaller circular disc shaped craft came and went.

The other extraordinary thing was it seemed to be alive, in that it seemed to breathe. Slowly it would become very, very solid — then gradually become almost invisible and I could see the stars in the night sky with only vague outlines of the craft remaining. It would then begin its materialization once more. The first thought that struck me was, Oh, so that's how they get about. They can go from one dimension to another and cover vast distances in space.

By this time I was sitting on the end of the bed watching this amazing event playing out before me. I felt no fear at all — just curiosity more than anything. This went on for about twenty minutes at the end of which the room became filled with a very bright light. I said —loudly "you're not taking me on board." The next thing it was 7 am and the sun was streaming into the room.

In the years since then I have often wondered if I should seek hypnotherapy to glean what took place during those hours of 3 am to 7 am on that day. Many researchers have told of lost time and no memory of anything from several hours to days and being awoken hundreds of miles from where they were prior to the event.

Everything is interconnected on many levels of our lives. No doubt alien life forms have interacted with humanity over all of our time as physical beings. In many myths and sagas gods are depicted in flying machines and warfare using what appears to be atomic weapons. This has been preserved in the records.

I have mentioned these 'encounters' in this narrative as all these experiences go into the woven pattern of my life. I am who and what I am because of this and my attitudes to them. We are indeed the sum of our parts — thoughts — actions, etc. It is said no thought, feeling or deed is not recorded in the Akashic records. It is sometimes hard to know (it is said) when researching someone if, in fact, something took place in their past or the thought was as far as it got.

No doubt there will be people who read this and whose immediate reaction is one of ridicule and totally dismissive, calling for the keepers at the funny farm to pay me a visit. So be it — they are free human beings who decide their own destiny as we all do.

My grandmother on my dad's side used to say "never judge anyone today because you never know what you will be doing tomorrow yourself."

CHAPTER SEVENTEEN

As I mentioned earlier, I had suffered for several years with an auto-immune illness which made my life very miserable and restricted. Also unbeknown to me I had a condition called "diverticulitis".

In June 2011 I suffered a huge internal bleeding which led to my death from loss of blood.

As I left my body and floated way above the city, I was accompanied by the same cloaked figure who featured in the dream with the ghost in the wooden room and the camera under the floor boards.

I said to him "Why is anyone afraid of death? It is marvellous. I feel so free." These are the same words a friend who had taken her own life in early 1990's said to me when she appeared that evening at the foot of my bed. (I was unaware until the next day of her death). She said it twice, "Richard I am so free." I said to her, "Helen — you look wonderful — so well." She said it again—then was gone. Anyway, I digress. I said to my 'guardian', "All the things I haven't finished — if they are worthwhile — someone else will do it. If not, then they are of no importance anyway." I seemed to drift into another realm and spoke with people whom I knew then but unable to remember who they were now.

I was there for what seemed to me a considerable time when the thought struck me. Who will look after my dog Nikki? In an instant I was back in my body. Somehow I rang the friend who I had tea with that afternoon and she phoned an ambulance.

It was the first overnight stay in a hospital for me in over sixty years — since I was five years old, having tonsils removed. It was fashionable at the time to do such procedures!

I was xrayed and had all sort of tests done with tubes inserted into my hands, etc. All very overwhelming.

About 3 am a tall young doctor came by. He was the gastroenterologist at the hospital. He introduced himself and said, "you have diverticulitis and have had a very severe bleeding—not uncommon. But you will be fine!"

Next morning an older version of the same doctor came to my bed — he introduced himself and said the very same words. I said, "But you were here last night." "No" he replied, "I have just come on duty."

It puzzled me for the next few days in the hospital before they conducted a colonoscopy. When I spoke with him I realised, here was a man with a genuine healing quality. No doubt as he slept he worked on other planes and interacted with patients on ours as well.

After all things were completed I was discharged a day or so later with the farewell greeting "You'll be OK for another 300K."

The following year I had a recurrence — and, although not as severe, I was readmitted. The doctor said, "This time we will find the tear in the colon and repair it." Which he did.

Two months later the autoimmune illness which was triggered by severe inflammation disappeared.

Three years later I am still well and after recent blood tests etc, given a clean bill of health.

I have recounted this saga — not so much for the medical side of it — but how the spirit world interacted during the drama. In a way I feel blessed by having gone through the experience.

I had often wondered to myself, how did I end up living so far away from all I knew and had grown up with? Again, synchronistic events lead us to be where we should be to experience these life enhancing transformations.

CHAPTER EIGHTEEN

There was one dream which occurred in the early 1990's which has stood out in my memory for years. I was debating whether to include it or not. It is so detailed and amazing I decided to include it.

It is set in an old colonial part of Africa and seemed to be in the recent past.

The Dream

I had returned to this area after many years abroad and, walking on the outskirts of the town, I came across a grand house set behind high walls. There were extensive gardens — in fact it would be several acres of beautifully laid out formal beds, trees and shrubs.

I remembered it from when I was young when the occupant lived his final days in solitary grandeur.

The gate was ajar just slightly so I could take a peek at this amazing garden which was very green and lush. This was in contrast to the rest of the town and surrounding area which had been in drought for several years.

I pressed the button, hoping someone would come out and perhaps let me explore the estate. No one did, so I took a few steps in — worried guard dogs might appear when they got scent of me.

No one was about at all and my eye got caught by a huge granite pyramid set in the lawns with four sleeping carved lions at each corner.

There were hundreds of white roses planted around its base. There was a plaque commemorating the owner and creator of the estate on one side. I do not remember his name. I did remember it seemed familiar at the time. He had been a big game hunter for most of his life and had amassed a considerable fortune. I seemed to 'know' all these details.

Everything had been created and built upon 'death'.

Perhaps the pyramid was symbolic — weighing many tons; it kept his spirit locked up in the earth.

The four lions were there to guard it and the roses to suppress the stench of death. I remembered the phantoms of the dead animals following the two American women into the dining room of the hotel in London in 1966.

My gaze was directed towards the beautiful Colonial mansion with spacious verandas on all sides.

There was no one about and after calling out several times, I opened the door to a vast room with handmade rugs on the polished boards and stuffed heads of dead animals on every wall. The furniture was of a solid wood and leather style possibly what one would see in the 1920's.

On the floor in front of an enormous fireplace was the coat, legs and head of a lion. I was so moved by this sight I picked up one of the front legs and held the paw in my hands. As I stroked it I thought — who could shoot and kill such a magnificent beast. I started to cry. To my amazement there seemed to be a warmth emanating from this dry, lifeless flesh. It seemed to grow in my hands. In what appeared to be a very short time the legs started to swell and become filled with life once more. I could even see bone and blood vessels with fur — all growing at an amazing pace. The body and head also were reforming into a living, breathing animal before my eyes.

The lion sprang to his feet — stood on his hind legs and gave out an enormous roar. He opened his mouth and bounded towards me. I thought — I have brought him back to life and now he will eat me! He licked me on the face with a tongue which felt like sandpaper — turned and sprang towards the door and, with another almighty roar disappeared into the grounds.

My first thought was to go to the museum and bring all those poor stuffed creatures back to life. A voice inside said, "No—as the museum is in the centre of town it would just create chaos for all concerned."

In the distance I could hear gun shots and much yelling. I thought "No—they are killing him once more!"

The people who were the caretakers of the estate were there with a crowd of townsfolk and another group who were dressed in 18th century garments.

Many were trying to shoot the lion but an unseen hand would deflect the gun prior to the trigger being pulled.

There was much agitation between the townsfolk and the religious group over a woman who had had an adulterous affair with someone outside of their community.

The deceased 'big game hunter' appeared before the crowd and called for calm. The lion sat beside him. He said to the crowd, "Do not harm this lion. Through this act of redemption and love by our visitor I have also been set free. Try to live in harmony from now on. My life was one of waste. Do not follow my example. It leads to loneliness and despair. I died a broken, unhappy man. Now I have been forgiven and can move on."

There is no doubt, many interpretations one could glean from this dream on many levels. There is the universal theme of redemption through love. There is also the contrast of the lush green estate against the drought and stricken area surrounding it. This is where the townsfolk and the religious cult live.

The women in both groups were no doubt suppressed in every aspect of their lives and almost 'owned' by their husbands. Wherever the feminine principle is suppressed in the world the life forces of the earth dry up.

The hunter represented masculinity out of balance. He rejected any tenderness and compassion in his life.

Nature strives for balance — never revenge.

I leave it to the reader to decide what if anything in this dream means to their own individual lives.

CHAPTER NINETEEN

Everything — every object — every living creature on this plane is interconnected. We form strong bonds with plants, animals and seemingly inanimate objects.

Clocks are very much associated with their owners and will often stop at the exact moment of death.

On two occasions I had experiences that involved clocks.

The first was in 1972 when I purchased a lovely 1920's mantle clock from a friend, and sent it off to be repaired at vast expense! It has a lovely chime and I still have it to this day.

When I purchased my home and gallery in Woolloomooloo my friend, Elizabeth who was very sensitive to the unseen world around us made a visit prior to the refurbishment.

When she entered the first floor area her first remark was, "oh there is a cranky old man at his desk over on the south side of the room. He is shuffling papers in a very agitated manner."

Several months later — after all the renovations — the clock was placed on the antique cabinet — possibly in the spot where Elizabeth had 'seen' the old man all those months ago.

A month or so later with my partner's parents visiting at the time, the clock was striking about 9 pm as I walked up the stairs to that level. The others were already in the room.

Without warning the clock flew fifteen feet across to the other side of the room and crashed to the floor. No doubt it was annoying to our resident 'old gentleman' so he threw it in anger. Luckily the case was not severely damaged and the mechanism was OK. The repair bill was not too horrendous.

We had also placed a beam operated buzzer across the front door to enable us to be alerted if there were clients entering the building should we be on another floor.

Every afternoon at 3 o'clock the buzzer would go off even if the door was open or closed. We tried turning the mechanism on at different times to see if it was some sort of timing fault. No matter what we did, if it was on it buzzed at 3 pm for years. Sometimes one would 'see' a figure go up or down the stairs out of the corner of one's eye. We got so used to it —we took no notice and the daily 'buzzer' routine became part of the fabric of our lives.

For some reason I never felt I should interfere in any way. It was as though I 'knew' not to go there. It was something that was out of my control.

The other incident concerning a clock began in 2004 on a recently deceased friend's birthday in August.

I had purchased the clock from Gary P. in 1990. He had found it in a shop in Boston USA on a trip the year before. It is of a very pleasing design and has a lovely bell chiming device. Only recently made but of a very high standard. I had talked him into selling it to me and upon subsequent visits over the years would always refer to is as 'my clock'.

He died in 2004 after several years of ill health, becoming a recluse and cutting himself off from former friends. I think he died in a very bitter frame of mind. I gave him his 40th birthday party in 1980 and nearly two hundred people came to the celebration.

At his funeral one could count the mourners on one hand.

His birthday was in August and on the exact day the clock stopped and started on its own several times. This went on for several years — both on the anniversary of his death in June and on his birthday in August.

It became very annoying — to say the least — as I was always having to reset the time. Otherwise the clock ticked away happily for the rest of the year.

During a visit by my clairvoyant friend Jean — she said to me, "there is a very angry, bitter man standing near you in the corner." Her description fitted Gary very well.

About four years ago — on the anniversary of his death — the clock stopped at 3.45 am. I looked at my watch so I could reset it, only to find my watch had also stopped at 3.45 that morning as well. Next day the clock was back to normal.

The following year these patterns repeated themselves and I got very angry. I said "Gary — if you don't leave the clock alone I will take it outside and smash it — I am fed up with this nonsense."

After I calmed down I spent some time telling him about the realm he was trapped in, etc. I asked forgiveness for anything I had done to upset him. If I had — it had never been done intentionally. I also forgave him for several incidents he had inflicted upon me over the years. From that time on the clock has behaved itself, except for a part that had to be renewed.

There is no doubt the dead are always around us in their own dimensions. When we think of them with love or even incidents in both our lives I am convinced they try to tell us something of their new state of being.

When my brother-in-law died in Queensland over a decade ago I was asked to give the eulogy at his funeral and cremation.

At the end of the service — just prior to the coffin being slid into the flames — I silently asked John if he was happy in his new abode and that the service in his memory was to his liking. To elicit an answer I said "John, if yes, make one of the three wreaths on the floor leaning up against the plinth or stand where his coffin is—to stand up and fall forward." I said "The one on the left." Then quickly said — or whispered "No, make it the one on the right." Which it did. There was an audible gasp from the mourners as it seemed to defy gravity — in the way it fell.

At the wake I told my sister her late husband was OK and happy, etc. As I was speaking with her another of my sisters, Janet came by and overheard what I was saying. She said, "When that happened I said to myself—Richard had something to do with that!"

As Jean Inness said in her book —"The dead never die."

CHAPTER TWENTY

The preceding chapters are the events — dreams — experiences which have moulded my life path. My own unique autobiography.

We can intellectualise on the meaning of our life and life in general forever. In my mind it is the 'deed', the actual experience that we take with us from this world when we die that is the core of the journey.

As I have said — every experience we have is unique in the whole universe — just like musicians have to keep practising until they master the instrument and bring forth the glorious sounds — drawing in the people to listen.

Beautiful sound is without a doubt integral to the very fabric of life and also reminds us of our true home in the spirit realms.

In the beginning was the word.

George Bernard Shaw is reported to have said "all great truths begin as blasphemies."

Most people hate change — they are content in the everyday routine of their lives. When a new way of seeing and thinking comes along it is resisted firstly by ridicule — then outright hostility before it becomes accepted into the fabric of our days. All of us suffer from varying degrees of neurosis on many levels in our personality. One has only to look at art, literature, music, fashion etc to see a best seller book of fifty years ago is virtually forgotten today and would be dismissed as totally irrelevant in our times and lives.

When that book appeared, it resonated with others on a similar wave length, just as fashionable artists and musicians do. As times evolve these various forms of neurosis metamorphose into some other manifestation. The best seller — top of the pops —whatever is almost regarded as an aberration by later generations.

Wisdom does not come with age — it comes from experience and knowing how to observe what that experience is teaching us — even illness symptoms are great teachers.

One of my favourite gems of wisdom was reportedly spoken by the great American Indian Chief, Seattle. He said, "when we spit on the earth we spit on ourselves." If people just held that saying close to their hearts — their lives would be transformed.

Truth — what is it? Science will promote mechanical thinking for one or two centuries—then along comes quantum physics which pulls the rug from under it all. Look at so called organised religion? How many innocent, free thinkers were burned alive because they presented mankind with a new viewpoint?

What began in the time of Christ — full of hope, love, understanding and tolerance degenerated into a system of control and regulation. They had the truth and no one was allowed to challenge it. In the twentieth century more people have been murdered —incarcerated and tortured by their own governments than in any other period in the history of the world.

Governments should just govern. Most today are about control and regulation on every level of our lives from mass medication to banning books to censorship etc, etc, etc. Some readers might object to my seemingly change of focus — I feel everything in this realm interconnects. We have chosen to be incarnate and we have to accommodate our lives to the prevailing regimes and period of history where we are.

The days of the monastic life are over. We have to adapt our spiritual life into the everyday chores of survival on so many levels.

Again — observing our actions and trying to see how they affect others by standing in their shoes is what I have elected to do.

Years ago I was discussing with a friend — what is truth. I heard myself saying the following: "Truth is hidden at the centre of a diamond. There are as many facets on that diamond as there are people on this earth. Looking through our own particular facet we observe our own unique version of 'The Truth'. No other human being sees our truth as we do. As we are unique—so too is our version of what we call Truth. The Truth we embrace will either free us or enslave us."

Sadly whilst we slumber through our lives — just reacting to events — we are more likely to be enslaved by 'our truths' which, in fact, are often manufactured by hidden forces controlling our lives and 'entertaining' us with 'Reality' TV — perpetual wars and non-stop violence.

Stalin is reported to have said, "ideas are more powerful than guns—we don't let our people have guns—why should we let them have ideas"!

Hitler said, "Terrorism is the best political weapon—nothing drives people harder than a fear of sudden death." (Still very apt for these times as well.) Also, he said he would remain in power whilst the people did not think!

Napoleon claimed the life of every citizen was his country's property!

Oh, I could go on and on about the cynical creatures who claim to be our leaders. Whilst we remain asleep and neglect to take responsibility for our own lives we will forever be enslaved.

Goethe was right. "Govern one's self. Never confuse freedom with licence."

Despite the foregoing, I see great hope for mankind as many people who have had near death experiences have often said as they left this realm they observed perfect justice at work. So often, when it appears to us that we exist in a realm where so called legal niceties seem to override true justice for the victims — it can often be the reverse.

All those scientists who create death machines — poisons and all sorts of life suppressing inventions will in a future life elect to undo the horrors they unleased upon the world.

Even the good one does may have to be dismantled, reversed or modified in our future lives. As with organised religions — philanthropic organizations etc all have their season —their relevance to the needs of humanity before decadence solidifies the once malleable, joyous, message at their birth.

When great thinkers and gurus founded movements that changed the lives of the followers — they linked their own karma to all these souls. It is a great responsibility. Do they do it in full knowledge of the obligation for generations it will impose upon? Every author links himself with the reader — often being bombarded with negative thoughts, even hate as well as the admiration of others.

It is indeed a great responsibility for any leader or new thinker who awakens these slumbering aspects in another's soul; what can seem to be a great liberation may confine in the future.

Even mundane things like choosing where one lives — i.e. a farm or an apartment — we create larger or smaller jails for ourselves which often become a great millstone once they pass their use by date.

In the future technology will dominate every aspect of our lives. Robots will dispense goods and services. Many individuals will be made redundant by this unstoppable avalanche of innovation.

Free energy will be universal — not without a great resistance from the so-called fossil fuel moguls. There will without doubt be great benefits but, again, the authority of the police state to monitor every moment of our day and night will be there. A great challenge indeed.

Some periods in my life were very bitter for me. At the age of fifteen I contemplated suicide by drowning. At the moment before I jumped, looking at the dark deep water, the thought came to me, why am I letting my father dictate my life? I will fight back on every level. He is only another human being like me—I don't have to react to his horrifying personality. I decided I would ignore him completely. From then on I never answered any question nor did I explain myself to him in any way whatsoever. I would arrive home late to avoid having to sit at the table and he would attack me, verbally, whilst I ate in the kitchen on my own. I said nothing. This went on for months at a time.

I was in control and very much empowered. He taught me a huge lesson — nothing shrivels an argument more than utter indifference to the opponent's ranting!

I know all that life has dished up on my plate is of my own choosing — whether now or at an earlier time. In many ways I am grateful, as my journey prompted me to turn inward and examine my own self. If I had not been born into such a dysfunctional environment would I have embarked on such a journey?

As I often say to friends who ask after my physical and mental well-being "I am completely adjusted to my maladjustments." In other words, I have accepted myself for who I am and not having to compare with others, their choices and mind set.

To sum up, I have created a philosophy based upon the following few words

Think with one's heart.
Love with one's mind.
Try to find some beauty in everything.
Is mankind's destiny beyond good and evil?

CHAPTER TWENTY-ONE

A SUMMING UP

I believe that philosophy is not just about what one thinks – it's about what one does.

It begins at the very heart of one's being. Our regime of eating habits; central desires and tastes even down to the clothes we feel comfortable in.

It is the 'wholeness' of our life. It is the rock we build our lives upon and that which leads to our inner happiness or misery. It depends if we have taken the time to lay down proper solid foundations.

Tolerance, an open mind and acknowledging that everyone in this world has a right to their own point of view (as you do yourself) (these are solid foundations).

It is never forcing your views on to others; they will enquire when they are ready as they have their own agenda to attend to. As I said, everyone is correct from their point of view. Hopefully one is not placed in a position where social engineering is the dogma of a regime you live under. Many might say "obey the law and you are above the law"; again if there is widespread corruption this road would prove fragile or difficult at best.

Writing this book was a necessary distillation of my own thoughts and experiences of a lifetime. It was important for me to clarify who I am. One could say it was written for me alone!

If others find something of value to add to their own life experience and vision – then that is a wonderful bonus for which I am grateful.

I never intended to impose my ideas onto others. I have chronicled my inner life to show how I was able to adapt and survive in this realm. By observing these experiences, making them truly conscious in my everyday life, has been for me an amazing journey – for which I feel blessed.

Even everyday chores like preparing a meal (be it for yourself alone or others), our attitude will be as important as the ingredients; perhaps even more so.

If one is angry, feeling frustrated, mean-spirited; [these feelings] will be reflected in the life forces of the food.

This has been shown by the pioneering work of Dr Emoto who demonstrated [these life forces]. He took one glass of water and poured it into three disks then proceeded to bless or curse [the contents]. He then froze the water and examined the water crystals. The blessed water created beautiful near perfect crystals. The indifferent water had nice crystals but far from that of the blessed ones. The cursed water displayed deformed and broken crystals.

He also [conducted the same experiment] with a pot of rice. After cooking, he placed the rice into three disks. Again he blessed one, cursed another and left the other untouched. After three weeks the blessed rice looked as though it was still edible. The indifferent dish had begun to ferment, whilst the cursed dish was black with mould. I urge the reader to enquire into his amazing research. I was alerted to this work by a scene in that extraordinary movie 'What the Bleep Do We Know?'

Water is life and I believe water has memory. There is vital life [full of energy and minerals] flowing [within] water that [emanates] from deep in the earth. There is also water devoid of everything except that its liquid and its wet! The latter when ingested will absorb energy from the drinker in its effort to restore itself.

I believe nature does not seek revenge; only balance. What is nature but a vast collective consciousness and as Carl Jung said our conscious mind is like a cork floating upon this sea of thoughts.

Our own little cork is on a journey through the time of this dimensions and our individualisation.

Perhaps we are emerging from a past where only a few were capable of seeing truly clearly. We are starting to see our true selves emerge from a fog of instinct.

All the buried experiences are being brought to the surface to be evaluated in the full light of day.

I believe we will all be forced to confront our portrait hidden in the attic and see for the first time how we have distorted our lives by our attitudes, thinking and actions.

Also as time goes on (and it seems to me to have speeded up - even young people are saying it!) we will have greater and greater difficulty in disguising our true feelings and intentions. It will be visible to all we interconnect with. Our portrait (painted over many lives) will more and more align with the physical form we inhabit on this Earth.

No doubt as the light within mankind burns brighter it will cast a much deeper shadow. In a sense this is mankind creating adversity to test and strengthen resolve.

These forces which no doubt will be external, or appear to be so, will place every obstacle in our paths to self-realization. These forces wish for man to be forever imprisoned in the material realm and to disconnect with our true spiritual home.

Politicians say "elect me if you know what's best for you. We will take care of you from the cradle to the grave. We will create laws to prevent every conceivable accident or horrible thing happening to you. If you are offended by someone's words or actions, we will punish that person", and so on and so on.

Freewill and all personal responsibility for one's life will be suppressed. Mankind could end up incarcerated in a world of political correctness. All spontaneity would be forbidden.

There are several forces at work. The Gods who have enjoyed control over man's destiny for generations may not wish to relinquish that power so easily. Yet as man's true destiny is freedom, some of them will no doubt work with mankind to achieve that end.

Nietzsche was very concerned for mankind; he saw God as dead. He was not making an idle statement. He could see mankind as a 'free force' with the power to destroy himself and the planet. Without the guidance of the gods and their interceding when times required it, mankind was and is now, on his own in a manner of speaking.

The political systems of the world over the last one hundred years have eroded ninety percent of man's right to forge his own path with promises of a brighter future. All have failed and will continue to fail until each individual desires cooperation and harmony with one's neighbours. Then truly man will begin to govern himself; thinking from his own higher nature and not from selfishness alone.

If a society has economic freedom – political freedom soon follows, as the former cannot exist without the latter. A free press (not infiltrated by vested interests and powerful corporations) would keep a nation truly informed. No famine has happened in the last two hundred years in a country with a free press. As I would hope, if nations form free trading treaties, the individuality of nations and their cultures are celebrated and not suppressed by central governments.

I could go on and on as we have made our lives so much more complex during my lifetime. Each new labour saving device has only enslaved mankind even more. There is no privacy. The challenges man faces are enormous on so many levels.

When I was a young man; life was simple and straight forward. There was virtually no problem with drugs and crime was usually one of passion. Today the world is so complex on so many levels; all created by man himself, his thoughts and actions.

This is indeed the age of the cinema. Cinema has shaped the world for more than books did in the past. The people who could read in 19th century Europe and America were in the minority. The film can be enjoyed and understood by all and has shaped our thinking, as television and radio do also. Hitler used radio and film for propaganda, mesmerizing the people into following him.

This slim volume, this tiny aspect of my biography, could be likened to a film where I am script writer, producer, director and cameraman of my life. A life like everyone else's; [a life that is] unique and guided by infinite possibility.

Once we adopt a philosophy gleaned from outside our own life experience, following rituals even following the life of Christ, marketed by a Protestant or Catholic 'brand', we give up our own free will and thought.

Christ is reported to have said …. "[we are] all Christ beings in the making and you will do even more miraculous things than I have done." He also is reported to have said "….. become as a little child or you cannot enter the Kingdom of Heaven." A child has no concept of intellectual complicated philosophical or religious belief. A child is just pure joy; open to all the wonder of the universe. All the child has is their few years on this planet to draw upon; even when they are brought up in horrible circumstances. The child still sees goodness in everything before we destroy that wonderful enquiring mind and make it conform to our version of the norm.

Even Buddha (who spent his life searching to find meaning) never sought to impose his teachings on anyone. It was his followers, who laid down the protocols which no doubt have fuelled immense benefits for Man, but again in some cases only enlarged his jail.

We all create our own jail by our attitudes, emotions and thinking. Two steps forward one step back seems to be the Universal dance of mankind.

Despite any negativity I have expressed, I am supremely optimistic for mankind's future. Wayne Dyer explained it very well when encountering argumentative people, he simply said "You're so right there," which in a sense they are, just as you are. If one just goes about one's life without intentionally hurting others, then all will go in diversity and harmony at the same time.

Our journey will take us all to ideas, places and experiences beyond anything we can ever glimpse in present times.

As I have always said whenever a dear friend (or even complete strangers) shed their earthly garments for a higher realm; "bon voyage – explore the possibilities one has started and perhaps one day we will all meet up again – fully aware of our heritage and potential."

Life is indeed a banquet on every level of our existence – even when it appears to be the complete opposite.

ABOUT THE AUTHOR

Richard J. King lives in a beachside suburb of Hobart, Tasmania with his 'whaskelly' wonder whippet Mister Bailey, who came into Richard's life four years ago after the passing of his beloved Boxer, Miss Nikki. Bailey is a source of great delight to all who meet him.

Richard started work while still attending school at the tender age of 12. He maintained his job as a chemist delivery boy until he was 15, then became an apprentice carpenter for a few months, before joining the Bank of New South Wales. He remained at the bank for 7 years before becoming an accountant for the British Overseas Airways Corporation (BOAC) in Australia. This job provided a great opportunity to travel worldwide.

Richard's love of the arts led to the opening of his own art gallery which specialised in original works on paper. Richard has also authored and published several books on various artists.

After 21 years he started a farm with his friend John Pick of King Pick Farm which produced cut flowers for export and local sale. The farm flourished for nine years but the bush fires of 2001/2 made him re-evaluate his life, prompting his move to Tasmania; a place he loved, having visited several times in late 1960's and 1970's with Murray Smith (who hailed from Burnie).

Richard is a music lover, an archivist and writer and as a Gemini always complaining that life has too many infinite possibilities.

This book is a chronicle of his inner life which has shaped and enhanced him, guiding him through turbulent times and laying the foundation for his own philosophical understanding of our interconnectedness and karmic journey.

www.ingramcontent.com/pod-product-compliance
Lightning Source LLC
LaVergne TN
LVHW091552070426
835507LV00010B/806